THE *Merry*
Nutcracker

THE *Merry Nutcracker*

A Christmas Story by

Marilyn Brown

Based on the Musical *The Merry Nutcracker*

BONNEVILLE BOOKS ™

Springville, UT

ISBN: 1-55517-828-6
v.1

Published by Bonneville Books
Imprint of Cedar Fort Inc.
925 N. Main Springville, Utah, 84663
www.cedarfort.com

Distributed by Cedar Fort, Inc.

Cover design by Nicole Shaffer
Edited by Janet Bernice
Cover design © 2004 by Lyle Mortimer

Printed in the United States of America
10 9 8 7 6 5 4 3 2 1

Printed on acid-free paper

Library of Congress Number: 2004113529

For the players who made
The Merry Nutcracker
come alive at the Villa Playhouse.

1

George Franklin was not what one would call a merry young man. He had always been serious, even in the cradle. But when he was eleven years old and the constable knocked on the door one afternoon while he and his mother were having tea and announced that his father's body had been found bobbing in the water at the quay, he developed an almost permanent expression of perplexity and determination in his brow. "Your father had many gambling debts," the constable said in a low even monotone while he sat with his round hat perched on his knee.

Indeed there were "gambling debts." When it was discovered his father had left payable notes of fourteen thousand, five hundred and twenty-three dollars and forty-five cents, his mother put the house up for sale, bought a sewing machine and a cheap flat at the end of Broad Street, and began to pay the debts while she eked out a living mending other people's clothes. Because no one else in her family lived in America, she knew there would be no help. Her only other child, a daughter from her first marriage—George's half sister Sadie—had long ago married a toymaker and gone to live in Bavaria. The mother and son had nothing to rely on but their own resourcefulness, which they were determined would get them through.

George, more like his mother than his father, was a persistent young man who was often head down with his hair in his face so that no one could see the unflinching scowl in his eyes. Joining his mother's crusade for economic freedom, he offered himself as a laborer on the waterfront. Every day at four in the morning until school began, he worked to pay his father's gambling debts. And every box he lifted, every rope he pulled, or knot he tied, he swore to himself he would never leave his own son to struggle so.

As he and his seamstress mother began to clear the debts, he studied steadfastly after school far into the night, until he became proficient at numbers and advanced to his secondary status with an award in mathematics. He became so skillful, that he began to attract attention. He was asked to give the valedictory address at their high school graduation.

In the meantime, a prominent banker, Mr. McDougal, of the Solidarity Bank of New York, whose young daughter attended George's school, happened to be present at the high school graduation to fulfill his commission as a member of the school board. As he listened to the serious boy's valedictory address, he was impressed. Though George spoke in an almost monotone soto voce, and—in spite of the hair in the boy's eyes—

there was a power in his delivery that forced Mr. McDougal, and everyone else in the congregation, to sit up and listen.

"I am an American," said the boy with the scowl hidden by a lock of his hair. "No greater words could be spoken by any man or woman on this earth. I believe in the lyrics, 'Oh beautiful for patriot dream, that sees beyond the years.'" He paused. "We shall stay a great country only as long as we give our best. Until 'all success be nobleness, and every gain divine.'"

After he graduated at age nineteen, George knew he must search for a full-time position. One day he just happened to enter the bank established by the astute business practices of his classmate Muriel's father. When he asked if there was any work, Mr. McDougal remembered that he was the young man who had stood so straight at the pulpit and had given such an inspiring address. He sat back against the slats of his wooden chair—which bent at the springs with a distressful noise at his girth—and put his fingers on his lips in a gesture of deliberation. "Ah . . ." he said. He looked off into the room as though it seemed possible he would forget the boy entirely. But it was only for a moment that George felt uncomfortable.

"Ahhh . . ." said Mr. McDougal. "You graduated with honors in mathematics?"

"Yes, sir," said George.

Mr. McDougal paused for another moment with his gaze averted to the window where the rising buildings of 1897 New York stood in his view. "I suppose you are looking for a position that will utilize your expertise in numbers? Perhaps accounting?"

George did not know what to say. "Yes, sir," he said, feeling a little clumsy.

Mr. McDougal looked thoughtful. When he finally spoke again, George felt nervous indeed.

"What I would like to know . . ." Mr. McDougal paused, "Is if the young man who adds columns and has spoken so eloquently about discipline and mastery, is also capable of wielding a broom?" When he finished speaking, he placed both hands on the arm rests of his slatted chair as though he were braced for a rocky ride on the New York, New Haven and Hartford Railroad.

Feeling disarmed, George quickly assured Mr. McDougal that he was not allergic to a broom.

Another long and uncomfortable moment passed until Mr. McDougal said, "Well, then . . ."

He studied George's face for a long time. "All right. I am willing to take a chance on you, Mr. Franklin. But first we'll see how you do with the broom."

George, an unusually dedicated, obedient, and trustworthy worker, became an astute apprentice of the bank. Sweeping and mopping proved to be a helpful study of the corporate structure. Finding the mathematical errors in the papers that fell to the floor, he began offering his services as an accountant. Soon, as everyone who knew him expected, he rose rapidly in the ranks of those employees who stumbled along with their lesser gifts. In 1900 he became a teller at the age of twenty-two, and at twenty-four an accountant in line as an assistant to the president, Mr. McDougal himself.

In his cubicle near the president's office, bending over his assignments with fixed energy, he was a study in single-mindedness. There were nevertheless occasions—though few and far between—when he looked up from his work. And through the hair that had fallen in his eyes, he could catch an occasional glimpse of someone passing his door.

It was not long in his new position before he caught sight of a taffeta sash, or the back side of a flowered hat. And he soon became aware that one of the passing figures was the girl from a much younger class in his school—a girl he had never much noticed through his scowl. But now he had begun to take notice of Mr. McDougal's daughter. He could not help but become aware that she often walked past his door on the way to see her father.

Soon George began arranging exits from his gruelling work with figures to make an assessment of another sort of figure. He often left his office at opportune times to get a drink of water, or take papers to the tellers. And one day, feeling quite bold, he took folders to the president's office when Muriel McDougal was present.

On one such day at the turn of the century, when Muriel was wearing a fragrance that seemed to intoxicate from a great distance, George stood in the hallway when she came out of her father's office. Though he had planned this "coincidental meeting," he very quickly found himself off balance. For, in the presence of a pink parasol, ruffled gloves, and pink hat with a small feathered bird sitting in a rosette of calla leaves, George could see he was acting like a fool. He tried to catch his breath. A cascade of shiny curls burst from behind her ear and fell in a charming twist down into the lace at her throat. He was barely able to speak, the sight was so disarming. He stammered a greeting.

"Do you remember me? Your class was younger . . ." he began. "We both attended the Emerson Smith Secondary School on Thirty-Fifth Avenue. I gave . . ."

Her response took him by surprise. When she laughed the sound traveled down his spine and shook his solar plexus so profoundly that he felt faint.

"Of course I remember you!" she laughed. "Silly. You were the one who always stood on the side while we played rugby in the playground. You always had your eyes in a book or on a paper adding up numbers." She nodded. "You gave the valedictory address." She tossed her head back. "And it was very good," she added, giving him a disarming grin.

As the weeks passed, George Franklin found himself in the hallway on many occasions. The two schoolmates became acquainted in a most stimulating way, until finally, George developed the courage to ask Muriel to dance with him at the church dances. And once or twice he bid high enough for her contribution at the box lunch socials.

Through the months of daring to step into a social dimension he had never before experienced and, finding it exhilarating, George never lost sight of what he had resolved was the primary obligation of his life—to make money. He soon became proficient at dabbling in the stock market, where he began to turn a few dollars into many dollars.

At his cherished mother's death in May of 1903, George was able to afford an unusually remarkable funeral, and shortly afterward an unusually elegant diamond ring which he presented to Muriel while she sat in the hull of a boat on the quay.

She looked like an angel under her parasol, which shed pink light on her glorious cheeks. "Oh, yes," she said in answer to his question, and when they leaped toward each other for an embrace, the parasol bounced out of her grasp and over the side of the boat into the water. The proposal might have ended badly, but for the hour they spent chasing and retrieving it. They found themselves so full of laughter and enjoyed so many kisses and embraces, that the mishap could only have been remembered as an historic one.

2

*T*wo years after their marriage began, a child was coming. And George was able—for a profit—to sell the tiny flat his mother had purchased years ago. With prices rising and the world warming up for what looked like a war in Europe, he realized now was the time to look for the house that he and Muriel would call their family home— the home of their dreams. When Muriel's father, Mr. McDougal, hinted that George's appointment as full partner in the Solidarity Bank of New York was imminent, he also hinted that a large sum of money would soon be available as a gift to his daughter and son-in-law for the down payment on the house they would soon inhabit and fill with grandchildren.

George flushed with excitement as he heard the news. With Mr. McDougal's generosity they could afford a large house on Long Island in the modern section, complete with carriage house, servants, and valet.

He was on his way to a meeting of the New York-New Jersey Port and Harbor Development Commission, a new organization designed to study the transportation and trade problems in the great Port of New York. The cab George rode in drove through a very old neighborhood near the waterfront and he noticed a "for sale" sign on a large old mansion clinging to the edge of the wharf, its huge windows and mansard roof gray with age and neglect. On one side of the house behind a stuccoed wall was an overgrown yard, crowded with large fruit trees. The gate to the house flaunted ornate iron rails and rococo pre-raphaelite angels and nymphs laden with vines.

It was not the neighborhood that attracted him. The area looked suspiciously rough, so close to the waterfront. And the viaduct of the Eastchester road and the vicinity of the industrial area lay not far beyond. But it was the shape of the house, and its orchard and gardens which won his fancy—the tall, ornate front, the size of the windows . . . and the wall—except for the side on the waterfront, where an elaborate French door allowed the house to view the boardwalk, there was an unimaginably superb wall around the rest of the house—tall and ornamented, and imposing in its beauty.

George began to turn many thoughts over in his mind. It was true that this was not exactly the area he and Muriel had in mind. It was an old neighborhood on a very short street with imposing old homes. There were two other homes on the street that looked so old that they might collapse at a hefty sneeze. But several of the other homes were still in excellent shape, as though they had passed from family to family, like treasured antique chairs. Though the area was obviously older, it was closer to the bank than Long Island, and closer to his new community interest in the New York-New Jersey Port and Harbor Development Commission meetings.

"This is a magnificent old house. It just needs work," George said to himself. "A private and magical place. And not far from my undertakings with the Harbor Commission." Right there and then he vowed to call the telephone number on the sign. By the time he urged the cab to continue toward his meeting, he had written the phone number in his daily record book, and said to himself, *with Father McDougal's kind offering, I could probably afford to pay for this house and own it free and clear.*

The thought tantalized him.

That afternoon he inquired about the house, and learned that it was only a third the cost of similar houses in the new neighborhoods of Long Island. Excited, he hurried to find Muriel at her parent's house, where she was picking strawberries in the garden. When she stood up to greet him, she reached up to put a hand on her large straw hat, and the strawberries began to roll out of her basket.

"What is it now, George?" With her cheeks rosy from bending over in the strawberry patch, she got up quickly because she could tell by his voice that he was excited about something, and she had learned to be careful of his temper, because he seemed always to be on the edge of some crisis or other.

"I want to show you a surprise," George said without

revealing what it was. He took her by the elbow, and though it was awkward to walk swiftly through the mounds and clods of the strawberry patch, they made their way swiftly to Mr. and Mrs. McDougal's house, where they told her father and mother that they would be gone for the afternoon. When they went out into the street, they found the hired carriage still parked in front of the house. He boosted his burgeoning wife into the carriage and took her that very hour to the neighborhood where the old house sprawled like a chess king on the waterfront.

The horses drew the hired carriage with a clip-clop down the short old street with the seventeenth century homes. "Well?" George said.

Muriel turned to look at the old houses. Some of them were mansions. "Here?" she said, not believing it would be a place she would ever live. "These are *old* mansions in an old part of town on the waterfront."

Not wishing to break it to her suddenly that this was exactly where he wanted to live, George refocused her attention ahead. "Do you see that beautiful old wall with the wrought iron gate down the road?"

Muriel saw it.

"Look at the tall black iron rails at the top of it and behind it, the fruit trees bending in the wind."

"Oh," Muriel caught her breath, feeling the excitement of her husband, and feeling some of her own. "Oh. It's beautiful," she whispered in a very low voice. "What is it?"

George cleared his throat and decided to plunge into the abyss. "It's a house we could pay for in full with our money, without worrying about a mortgage forevermore. A house with a garden and fruit trees already blooming and bearing apples and pears. It's a home we will love always. At least I hope you could love it always, Muriel, as I feel I could love it—even without seeing it on the inside. For I feel it is speaking to us—to our very hearts."

"Oh," Muriel said. She shifted in the carriage seat.

"We will have our sons here. There is a waterway near the road that leads to the quay. They can make boats of old leaves to sail to the waterfront. They will grow up loving the sea. They may climb the apple trees and build treehouses in the branches."

Muriel seemed very quiet. "It looks old and empty."

"We will fill it with many children and there will be laughter and singing. The gardener and maid can live in the small apartment at the back over the carriage house." George led her forward to the iron gate, which was locked. So they walked around to the boardwalk and across the grass to the side of the house where there was no wall, just the beautiful ornate French doors that swung out onto the lawn. Shading his eyes, George peered into the wrought iron lattice work over the French doors. Inside, they could see a stately room with a high ceiling decorated with rococo swirls of plaster and medallions. Cupids were painted at intervals pinching a very realistic blue satin sash against the cornices. Though there were cobwebs everywhere, and the floor was littered with screws and flattened boxes, the tall windows at one side of the large room let in a filtered light that played in patterns on the inlaid wooden floor. George could hear Muriel's breath as she breathed in.

"Oh," she said. "It's beautiful."

George smiled. They made an offer on the house that very afternoon.

That night both of them dreamed about the old mansion, the ornate medallions above the tall windows, the mansard roof.

It was the house of their dreams.

3

Without seeing the property, the McDougals listened carefully to the description their young daughter and her husband gave to them, and rejoiced in the prospect that they would be able to pay for the house free and clear. It would cost twelve thousand, seven hundred and forty eight dollars and thirty-two cents. George had saved three thousand and the McDougals had presented them with ten. There would be enough to hire painting and gardening, and also a girl.

For some time Muriel had wanted to hire a girl to help them in the flat, and now that the baby was almost due, she had inquired around for someone who might be available. On a Saturday afternoon, while George and Muriel were working with the painters and carpenters of the new house, a young woman came across the boardwalk to the French doors. She was carrying a valise, knocking it against her legs. Her wool stockings were very loose, and her coat looked worn. The girl's huge crop of blonde hair was tied up in back like a bouquet of straw flowers on her head, and her face was a happy one.

"One of my friends at the bank read a notice that you needed help at your house," she said, introducing herself. "If you'd give me a chance, I could show you how much help I can be."

Muriel, skeptical, wanted to see letters of recommendation. George turned to his wife. He had been giving instructions to one of the painters named Peter who was about to paint out the blue sash in the great room. He said, "Let's try her, Muriel. It can't put us out to give her a try. If she doesn't work out, she doesn't work out, and we can let her go."

Muriel asked the young woman many questions. She was from Ardoyne in Ireland and had barely come to the United States of America. The girl was the oldest in a family of twelve children, and her parents had purchased passage for her so she might work and send money back to feed the many mouths that must be fed. While she talked, the young woman moved her feet in what looked like a little dance. She turned from side to side, sometimes abruptly enough to toss her skirts in the opposite direction. She looked off into the tall windows and across the quay with a distracted glance in her light blue eyes.

"I know how to take care of babies," Marietta promised with firmness in her voice. "I took care of me mum and all the babies while she had another."

It seemed she had very little schooling. But Marietta did know how to read as she proved when she promptly read the painter's bucket, "Thomas Jones, Incorporated."

"All right," Muriel said, knowing she did not have much

time left until she would be down with the birth of her child. "You may live in the little apartment above the carriage house." She paused and made a last-minute assessment of Marietta before she spoke again. "We will pay you a small salary that will increase only if you prove yourself worthy."

Marietta's face lit up with a large smile. She had even white teeth which looked like a row of pearls.

"Thank you, mum. You will not be sorry."

Marietta climbed the carriage house stairs with the valise still knocking against her dancing legs. She was in the new house cleaning up after the carpenters and painters before Muriel could turn around and say, "Let freedom ring."

4

he Franklins moved out of the flat and into the refurbished new home three days before Muriel began to have sharp labor pains. Finally in their beautiful new surroundings, George thought Muriel would rejoice at their good fortune and happily decorate the premises, singing little songs. But it was not to be; Muriel began to feel dreadfully ill. She did not want to stay in the bedroom, but begged George to bring her down into the great room where, curling up on the settee, she fell into a rigid fetal position, gasping for air.

"Muriel?" George was sick with worry. "Are you having the baby? Talk to me."

When she looked up at him, her eyes were crusty with dried tears. She could hardly speak. "I don't know what's wrong, George. I wonder if every mother feels this way."

When he held her hand, she clasped him back so tightly that her nails bit into his flesh.

"This is not right," he said. "I'm going to call your mother."

Muriel's mother now lived far away and visits had to be planned. When George finally got her on their new telephone he asked, "Does it always hurt this much?"

Muriel's mother sounded small and tinny on the other end, like a far away tunnel. "Yes, it always does."

"Should I call the doctor? Should she go to hospital now?"

Mrs. McDougal was quiet on the other end of the line. She did not know what to say. "I'll come as fast as I can. Usually the first labor takes a long time. Don't rely on the doctors here. Call a doctor in your own neighborhood who can see her right away." The Franklins had been using Mrs. McDougal's doctor for years. Perhaps it was time to search for someone more accessible.

George put the telephone receiver in the cradle and sat for a few moments trying to sort things through. Marietta came from the kitchen bringing hot cloths and basins of water. On one of her trips, George watched her arrive and suddenly, an idea came into his head. He would send Marietta.

"Marietta, thank you for bringing the water. I think we'll get along all right for a while, so I want you to go out and ask around for a doctor that might be close by. When you find one, please go and get him quickly." He began to turn back to Muriel, but added one last admonition. "And be careful to stay away from the ruffians that frequent the waterfront. Keep your distance from them and only ask around among the neighbors."

"Yes, sir," Marietta said. She made a nice little curtsy, her white apron brushing the tops of her ankle stockings. "Yes, sir, I will, sir." Marietta whipped the apron off in one stroke and went out the French doors onto the quay.

George sat with Muriel and did not go into work. He pressed her brow with warm water and tried to get her to sip soup from a spoon, but she wouldn't open her mouth. Her brow was in a sweat and her lips tightly closed.

It was a long time before George saw anyone come across the boardwalk. When he saw a shadowy shape, he could only hope it was the the doctor and not some vagrant who might have accosted Marietta, or some of the undesirable youth who wandered about near the water.

The dark figure was large and imposing in his tall hat, carrying a black case and walking as though he were going to a fire. Marietta hurried to reach the French doors ahead of him. She opened them with a flourish and ushered the man in.

"He lives down the street from you," Marietta said, "in the beautiful brick house with the cut lawn." She turned to him and smiled. "This is Dr. Robert Kendall, and he has taken care of patients in this area for years."

After she had delivered her message, Marietta whisked the basin of cold water into the kitchen where she asked Peter—who had begun working for the Franklins as their handy man—if he would please fill it with hot water again.

"Dr. Kendall," George rose from the settee where his wife lay like a small dried onion under a heap of afghans. He extended his hand. "I am so glad you're here. She isn't feeling well at all. I hope there is something you can do."

Even before he spoke to George, Dr. Kendall put his hand on Muriel's head to see if she had a fever. He pulled a stethoscope from the black case and placed the bell on her chest. "She has some obstruction in her breathing," he said with authority. "I am afraid she has a high fever, and perhaps . . ." he paused, as though testing George with his words. How much could this new young husband take? "Perhaps an infection . . ."

George felt the words cut through to his very stomach. He raised his eyes to the large man. "I will pay anything." He thought about how he had paid everything for the house. Yet, if Muriel should die, everything they had sacrificed for the house would not count. There would be nothing. He felt his legs shake for a moment, and then he turned away from the doctor and his wife at the settee. He walked to the windows of the French doors and looked out on the quay. He said a silent prayer in his heart, "Dear God, please, don't take Muriel. Oh, please help her and the baby to make it through. I plead with you. If you will protect them for me now I will protect them the rest of their lives. I will not ask much of you. Please, dear God, I ask you, please."

The doctor told Marietta what to do—to put cold compresses on her brow, not hot. She was to drink water even though she did not want it. She was to take a small amount of quinine to kill the infection, and she was to rest. She had suffered some false labor. When the labor pains reoccurred, Marietta was to fetch him immediately and he would come, for Muriel was a very small-boned, slight girl with a small birth canal, and there might be a chance he would have to be cut the baby out of the womb.

George felt his heart skid in his chest. His hands began to shake. After the doctor left, he sat at his wife's side as convulsive sobs shook his frame. Yet he swallowed the tears back, not willing to worry Muriel with his own anxieties.

He held her hand and as he gently rubbed it said, "It's going to be all right, Muriel. We must have faith. Faith can heal us. Just faith. Prayers and faith. We must believe God will bless us."

5

or several days the Franklin family seemed paralyzed with fear. Mr. and Mrs. McDougal, who were anxiously worried about their daughter, visited often. Dr. Kendall also came several more times without waiting for Marietta to call. From time to time he had charity patients at the wharfside—families with drunken fathers who must rely on government funds—so he stopped in to see his new patient, too.

On this visit, the doctor squatted down beside Muriel on the settee, and held the thermometer in her mouth while she struggled for air. "Mrs. Franklin, don't leave us," he said. "Your baby is coming soon and you don't want the child to grow up without a mother."

Muriel nodded weakly and took her medicine.

In a week, they knew the time had come. Marietta called George on the telephone and he came back from the bank immediately, not even waiting for President McDougal, who came with Mrs. McDougal shortly thereafter.

Doctor Kendall was already in the great room with Muriel

on a large table he had fashioned out of an old door. Marietta was bringing water, and the house painter, Peter, was pounding nails into the legs of the table to give them more stability. Muriel was sobbing and screaming, and the sound rent George's heart.

When the doctor saw George, he lowered his eyes to Muriel. "I'm so sorry, Mr. Franklin, but I find it necessary to cut . . . to make an incision." He paused then, his next words low and piercing. "It may mean she will never be able to carry another child."

George stood without moving. There was something about the word "cut" that tore into him with a fierce power. He could feel his legs shaking. "If you think we must," he said, barely. The doctor turned toward Peter and Marietta and began to bark orders while Muriel's pitiful screams filled the great room.

Marietta knew what to do. She had helped with many births before, suffering the pains and cries of her dear Irish mother. "We must have constant boiling water for the instruments," she said. "Peter, if you will keep the water boiling, I will take care of the instruments and the child."

George watched the activity around him, wishing he could disappear. He held his wife Muriel's hand. "It's all right," he said bravely. "The doctor will take good care of you."

The doctor administered the ether and Muriel became unconscious as George still held her hand. He insisted on staying with his wife and watching attentively while the doctor performed the miracle. Out of the clean sheets piled up around

Muriel, there was soon a short cry. The doctor held in his hand a small wrinkled child.

George leaned forward.

"It's a girl!" Dr. Kendall whispered. He brought the child over to George, who looked at the little body struggling to breathe. Dr. Kendall cut the cord, tied it, and gave the baby to Marietta, who washed off the chalky white coating with a clean cloth.

"Oh, she's beautiful," Marietta whispered. "Her skin is as clear and delicate as the petal of a flower." She wrapped the baby in clean gauze and attended to the afterbirth. Peter, a swarthy fellow who had taken to Marietta when he first saw her, made himself useful and ran in and out with more hot water.

They had both wanted a son, but if it happened to be a girl, Muriel had wanted to name her Clara after her own mother. George peered over into Marietta's arms and looked for a long time into the infant's face. She had stopped crying. "Clara," he said softly, "you are so tiny." He thought she looked like a very small bird who had just broken out of an eggshell. He didn't really think she was very pretty, but she *was* alive.

While the doctor returned to the task of repairing Muriel, George said a silent prayer of thanksgiving to God for saving their lives. He washed his fingers in the hot water, dried them, and touched Clara's little fist. Tears came to his eyes. "Little Clara, we're glad you have arrived."

6

lara was never a very healthy baby. The doctor said she had been born a little too early to develop her lungs fully. But if she had once been as ugly as a tiny bird just out of its shell, she soon grew into an amazingly beautiful child. Her fragility only enhanced her beauty—her hair was as light and airy as gauze, and the color of sunshine. The skin on her cheeks was so thin and delicate that one could see the blood below them pumping hard through her veins. She was so exquisite of form and face that she reminded visitors of a china doll. Her fingers were so slender, so delicate, that George could not look at them without an ache in his heart, and without often revisiting his promise, that he would protect her from the ravages of the world. He said over and over again to himself that she would be safe with him. Nothing could enter their lives to destroy this most miraculous child, he simply would not let it. He was uncomfortable when people came over to see Clara, and he would not let them come close for fear of breathing germs, or touching parts of the house with contaminated hands. When

Muriel wanted to send letters to her friends and relatives to announce Clara's birth, George went over her list carefully, and asked her to cut it in half. He insisted that there not be a lot of people coming in and out, and especially any who had young children who might bring infections. He himself sent only one announcement—to the only relatives he knew who were still living—his father's sister, Aunt Sadie, and her husband Uncle Harold, the toymaker who lived in Bavaria.

Except for going to church on Sunday, George and Muriel stayed very close to home. The Franklins sent Marietta and Peter out to do the shopping, which they hurried along as much as possible, hoping to escape serious mishaps. Once or twice Peter had been approached by a band of young brigands on the quay and robbed of his wallet. If the thieves took his money while he was on an errand for the Franklins, George often paid the damages.

George had many other problems too, of course—plumbing repairs, electrical problems, and ice that formed on the horses and carriage. But for the most part, there were long periods of cozy home life in which George kept his wife and child safe from the outside world.

Occasionally a girlfriend or two came to see Muriel, or a friend from church. Or friends from the neighborhood dropped in to say hello. Dr. Kendall's wife Sarah brought hot soup in a tureen once in a while, and Mrs. Jane Sawyer stopped over to help Muriel when she was weeding the garden. Otherwise,

Muriel and the little girl kept out of harm's way.

Both new parents watched with hope and delight as their darling child grew into a beautiful young girl. Though still delicate, subject to the vagaries of illness in all kinds of weather, the little girl seemed to be very happy, and driven to express her joy in dancing and singing. When Muriel's parents passed away, they left her a music box which was one of her favorite toys. Playing the music box a thousand times, she wrote several little songs to go with the tune.

But lately, sometimes in the middle of her singing, Clara began to cough. Sometimes the cough shook her so much that her little body would thrash about in defeat. Then Marietta would fetch Mrs. Franklin and they would lean over the little girl in great anxiety, holding her and soothing her until she could breathe again.

As the years passed, Clara continued to have the same serious trouble with her breathing. Gasping and coughing, crying out with terror, she fought for air. These spells, of great concern to George and Muriel, continued to keep them wary of any outside activity. They enclosed the house, hoping to check any source of infection. Only rarely did she go outside, perhaps in the garden for a few moments, and under strict supervision. But when she went outdoors, the spells seemed to grow worse. They asked Dr. Kendall if she might be developing allergies. They wondered if they should take her to a specialist at the Mayo Clinic. But Dr. Kendall assured them that she may grow out of the problem when she got a little older. He gave her medication that helped to shorten the length of the spells. So the Franklins decided to wait.

They grew hopeful as she turned seven, eight and nine, and the spells seemed to grow less and less staggering. Things looked much better for the little girl, until she reached the age of eleven when something serious happened. For some reason no one could understand, she became listless and ill. The spells returned and increased.

When Dr. Kendall was called to the house, he did not seem concerned. But Muriel and George were terrified by Clara's lethargy. As a small girl, she had danced about, laughing and singing, cradling her dolls, and reading aloud from her books. Now it was as though, tired of the spells which had dogged her, she had given up completely. She lay on the couch all day, or sat in one of the window seats that flanked the French doors opening up onto the grass that sloped down to the boardwalk. Sometimes she sang plaintive songs for hours. Often she just sat and looked out on the quay at the children playing on the waterfront.

George and Muriel watched as their daughter seemingly slipped away from life. They were frantic, wondering what to do. They brought Dr. Kendall in as often as he would come, but the good doctor seemed to be as stumped as they were. "There is no reason," he said, "that her condition should have slid into reverse. I can't understand it, though I will prescribe some laudanum for the spells." The medicine helped . . . but only a little.

7

efore the Christmas of 1917, the weather turned seriously cold in October. Clara woke up one morning and had two spells within an hour of each other. As she sat on the couch in the great room, she bent her head over the edge, her breathing ragged and laborious.

George held Muriel's hand. "I am beside myself." His voice cracked. "Muriel, I don't know what more we can do. The doctor doesn't think it's asthma. And the bank ... we can't move anywhere to any other climate if it is."

Muriel was trying to be strong. "I want to have faith," she whispered. "Let's pray that God will step in and give her better health, or that we'll finally understand what it is that bothers her."

George wanted to have Muriel's faith. He wanted to believe, but Clara's illness had begun to threaten the very foundation of their home. "One element of faith is taking steps to solve our own problems," he told his wife. "I think we should begin to investigate the Mayo clinic. Remember, the doctor told us that they might have some answers there . . ."

Muriel lowered her head for a moment before she spoke quietly. "I want to see her well," she whispered, "and I will do anything. If the doctor says the clinic could possibly make a diagnosis, at least let us try."

They had heard of some new tests that could be given to detect asthma, or other respiratory diseases. Beside themselves with worry, Clara's parents made tentative plans to take her to the clinic so they could be back in time for Christmas. If they could find out what was wrong, and if there was a possible cure, it would be the best Christmas present ever.

They wrote to the clinic and received a confirmation of their reservation. A doctor at the clinic wrote a warm letter inviting the parents to stay in a house near the clinic which furnished meals as well as pleasant rooms with a view of the city.

However, one morning two weeks before they were to go, another letter arrived, an unusual letter. It was a large envelope embellished with flowers printed on parchment. When George took the missive out of the mailbox, he turned it over and over in his hands before he opened it, almost afraid of what it might mean. He carried it into the house quickly, as though it would explode. Muriel came to his side to see what he had found.

"Those are the most unusual stamps I have ever seen," he said. "I can't read the return address. It looks like Bavaria."

"Bavaria!" Muriel exclaimed. "Remember?"

For a moment George could not remember.

"Years ago, when we sent the announcements of Clara's birth, you included your half-sister in Bavaria! I think her name was Sadie. And she was married to the toy maker, Harold Drosselmeyer!"

George was stunned. At last he remembered. "My own half sister," he said quietly. "But they have never written to us. I supposed our announcement had never reached them." He began to open it. "Sadie. Clara's Aunt Sadie."

As he began to read the letter, Muriel noticed that Clara had come down the stairs and stood at the kitchen door. She was still in her nightgown, wearing thin pink knitted slippers. Holding a blanket in her arms, she did not enter the room, but waited to listen. Marietta rushed to her and helped her to put the blanket around her shoulders. She did not cough. But she put her finger to her lips and said, "Shhh" to Marietta, because she wanted to hear what had happened. Even Marietta stopped to listen.

Dear George,

> *You will wonder if we ever received the news that you had a baby girl eleven years ago, but we did not receive the announcement until last year. It was always on its way, but we have been moving around. And now we are coming to New York City this Christmas on business, and we want to see your little daughter. We will be there on Wednesday, December twentieth. We*

have your address. We will find you. Cheerio!
Your true sister, Sadie.

When he finished reading, George looked at Muriel. "They're coming here!" he said.

Muriel sighed. "Oh, George!" She took the letter from George's hands and sat on the settee, reading it over and over again. Finally, she let it fall into her lap. "What are we going to do about going to the clinic?"

George was speechless for a moment. He turned toward the window that looked out over the quay. "It's impossible," he said. He stood for a few more moments.

Marietta vanished, feeling the tension in the air. She must have gone into the kitchen, for they could hear her banging the pans and pots about.

"We will write to the clinic and tell them to cancel." The hall rang with the tenor of his words.

"Oh, George. We had hoped. . . ." Muriel began.

"There's nothing else we can do," George said slowly. "We will pray that Clara will feel better. Sometimes miracles *do* happen!"

As they spoke, a small voice came from behind the door.

"Who is coming?" Clara asked, as she came into view and stood in her white nightgown, her blond curls wispy around her head. She looked like a small ghost.

Muriel looked at George, "Oh, little Clara!" She ran to her daughter and put her arms around her. "Darling, your father's sister Sadie and her husband want to come for Christmas, but we are worried about your spells. We wanted to take you to a clinic, but we will have to wait for that now."

"I'm getting better," Clara said in a weak voice.

George and Muriel looked at each other.

"Yes, I am, Papa," Clara squeaked.

"I don't know . . ." George began.

"Well, I am glad your Aunt Sadie is finally coming," Muriel smiled. She put the letter on the table. "We can put them in the room three doors down from Clara's, on the far end of the hall. I am sure they will be quiet. They will understand she cannot lose her sleep."

Muriel read the letter again, her hands touching the soft paper. "No matter how ill our little girl is, we must be hospitable. These are your relatives . . . the only ones still living. We must be glad they are coming, and we must give them a nice dinner party. We can invite a few well-chosen friends."

8

A week later Clara had another series of spells. They seemed more damaging than ever before. George and Muriel sent Peter for Dr. Kendall, and when he came both of them stood together in the great room while the doctor wrote out a stronger prescription for their daughter's laudanum. The parents clung to one another tightly, as though their love for each other might help keep their dreams from dissipating into thin air.

While they watched the doctor wield his pen, Marietta came in and out of the room asking questions, for Christmas was almost upon them. There were many things to get ready for the guests and the dinner party only a few days away. The Franklins invited some of the couples from the neighborhood, including Dr. Kendall and his wife, to come for dinner on Friday night, December twenty-first to meet George's aunt and uncle. Today was Tuesday. Sadie and Harold would arrive soon. Some of the ladies of the neighborhood had promised to come and decorate the house, but now the worst seemed to be happening.

"I have never seen her like this," George said.

"I don't think we ought to go ahead with the plans for the party," Muriel said.

Dr. Kendall looked up from his pen. "Oh, no. I would go ahead and have the party. I'll call in the prescription for the laudanum, and that might help. But some activity in the house, some singing and dancing may do her good." He put the pre-scription in George's hands and closed his bag. "You haven't been able to have any parties all these years. Besides, my wife and I were looking forward to it. No. Let's try to go ahead with the party. If Clara is really down, she can stay upstairs in her room. I don't think it will hurt anything."

Muriel bent her head into her hands and began to sob quietly. "If anything should happen, I could not bear it."

Though there was a feeling of anxiety throughout the house, the Franklins and their helpers kept busy decorating for the party and preparing the last minute details. Marietta opened the boxes of holly Peter had fetched, risking a trip to a farmer several miles out of town. When he had driven the carriage across the road, some of the urchins at the waterfront had tried to rob him again, but he threw them off this time.

As he brought the boxes of holly into the carriage house, Peter sang his favorite songs at the top of his voice. Several of Muriel's friends came over in the afternoon on the day Aunt Sadie and Uncle Harold were to arrive and offered to help put up the garlands of holly around the big room.

Even Clara was excited about the decorations.

All would have been well if she hadn't had another spell. From her bedroom, Clara tried to hold back her coughing, because she knew her mother would not let her go downstairs to see the ladies decorate the room if she had a spell. She buried her little face in the pillows on the bed and coughed and coughed. When she heard the doorbell ring, she sat up, but she coughed again as she heard Marietta answer the door.

"Your friends are here to help decorate for the party, mum," Marietta called to Muriel in the kitchen.

Clara heard her mother's voice. "Oh good. Get the boxes of holly, Marietta. And check on Clara while you are upstairs."

While Marietta came up the stairs, Clara could hear the ladies in the foyer. They were trying to talk low to each other, but Clara could hear them.

"If only her daughter wasn't so sick."

"Clara's sick?" Mrs. Liza Felton peered around the room, and noticed trays of medicine. The other ladies had known about Clara's illnesses, but Mrs. Felton had never been in Muriel's house before.

"She has these bad coughing spells," Mrs. Sarah Kendall, the doctor's wife, nodded.

Muriel quickly came through the kitchen to greet the ladies. "I'm so glad you're here! Thank you so much for coming to help me."

When she saw Muriel, Mrs. Liza Felton expressed her

concern to her. "Sarah mentioned your daughter's coughing. Have you tested her for asthma?"

Jane Sawyer, a lady from a house down the block asked, "Have you ever thought of moving to a dry climate?"

In the midst of the sudden interest of the women, Muriel tried to remain calm. She stood very still, but she began to twist her hands together.

"No, George does not want to move." She waited for a moment. "We were about to take her to the clinic, but—"

"—But you had to stay when you found out George's aunt was coming from Europe," Sarah filled in when she saw that Muriel was having difficulty. "I am praying that my husband can help her to grow out of this, Muriel. If we get through this party, he can help you get to the clinic."

The women were gracious and did not pursue the difficult subject further. Instead, they complimented Muriel on the beauty of the room, the paintings, and the furniture. When Marietta came in with the boxes of holly, they laughed and sang, hanging garlands on the cornice and draping others about the windows and tables. They took all of the ornaments out of the boxes and hung them on the tree. Muriel hurried about with her friends, genuinely making an effort to put her worries behind her.

As the women finished up in the room, Muriel went back into the kitchen to retrieve some ornaments Liza Felton offered to lend them for the tree. While she was gone, Sarah Kendall happened to glance to the top of the stairs. Clara, dressed in her white nightgown, stood wide-eyed on the landing, holding her doll against her shoulder. Slowly she came down the stairs.

Sarah hurried to her with concern in her voice. "Clara, are you all right?"

Jane followed Sarah. "Should you be down here, Clara dear? Your mother may not like it."

Liza, who had never seen the little girl before, smoothed her hair with the palm of her hand. "You're a beautiful little girl," she said warmly. "But maybe you should lie down on the couch before you catch a draft."

The women fussed over Clara, helping her to climb on the settee and bring the afghan up to her chin. Because Muriel had not come back into the room, the ladies left, quietly chatting with one another. The room was suddenly so quiet that Clara closed her eyes and drifted into an unsettled sleep.

9

he evening of Sadie and Harold's scheduled appearance had finally arrived. The Franklins knew exactly when their train would be coming in, but when George and Muriel came down the stairs to go to the train station, they were surprised to see Clara fast asleep on the settee. Muriel hurried to the bottom of the stairs to cover her with the afghan which had drifted to the floor. But George was clearly concerned. Throwing his overcoat over his shoulders, he began to walk heavily toward the door. "This isn't the best place for her," he said in his lowest voice.

Two hours had passed since Muriel's friends had left. Clara had been asleep for two precious hours without a spell. Except for some noisy laughter and skirmishing out on the quay, the house had remained dead quiet.

George went to the sofa and looked around the room. "It's colder down here with the door opening and closing. I didn't know she came down into the front room. Why is she down here, Muriel?"

"I guess she fell asleep after the ladies left," Muriel answered softly. "She tires so from coughing, I'm glad when she sleeps at all."

George put his hand on Clara's tiny brow. "She has a slight fever, but I realize she hasn't been sleeping well. If you give instructions to Marietta to watch her carefully, I suppose . . ."

George and Muriel put on their coats as Marietta hurried to take George's hat and umbrella off the rack. She brought them to him quickly, and he flung his wool scarf around his neck. As he tightened it around his throat, he stood for a moment, alerted by a noise outside the French windows that looked out on the quay. When he walked to the windows, he watched for a few moments. He was right, there *were* people out there. A group of ruffians were running on the waterfront. The clamor was deafening. He shook his head.

"Just those kids," he said. "Having a good time. Let's hurry."

Muriel turned to speak to Marietta, using her most serious voice, knowing Clara's very life depended on this girl's care while they were gone.

"If she has one of her spells, Marietta, call the train station," Muriel said. "We'll be right home. Uncle Harold and Aunt Sadie should be waiting for us. Don't forget her medicine."

"In the worst case, give her the double dose of laudanum," George said.

"It's a good thing Dr. Kendall will be here tomorrow," Muriel said thoughtfully.

As George glanced outside again, he stared numbly at the young people tussling and whooping on the quay. The sight of his ill daughter sleeping on the settee and the activity on the wharf troubled him for a moment.

"We needed a dozen children," he said softly.

Muriel looked toward him, startled. They had promised each other not to mention it. Ever. Her eyes began to fill with tears. "Please, George, you promised." She put her fingers on his lips. "I wanted them, too."

George continued to keep an eye on Clara and another on the young people outside the window, until he saw more clearly what they were doing. Peter ran up to the house, his shirt torn out of his trousers, and his hair standing up in huge spikes on top of his head.

"Oh, my goodness, Peter! What has been going on?" George exclaimed. He held the door open as Peter ran toward them, limping over the doorstoop. The young boys who had roughed him up were backing away from the house.

When Marietta heard the clamor, she ran from the kitchen with a towel in her hands. "What on earth! Oh Peter! Peter!"

Peter was bleeding. "I know it's true! Somebody hires those kids to steel your money and rough you up."

"They hire them?" George asked.

Peter was out of breath. "That's what happens. The gangsters pay the kids a percentage. And I had last week's pay in my money belt! Didn't do me any good to keep it close."

Marietta placed the towel against Peter's wounds. "Oh, Peter!"

George pulled the scarf from his neck because of the heat. "That's why they build safes in banks, Peter," he said in a low chastising voice.

"They've robbed banks before," Peter protested.

George felt disgusted. "I'm sorry, Peter. Maybe someday you'll join the rest of the civilized world."

George turned away and took Muriel's arm, noticing the young boys still on the edge of the lawn outside the French windows. They were standing behind some lilac trees at the edge of the quay.

"You brought those kids right up to this door! Heaven knows what will happen now."

Muriel checked the grandfather clock. "We need to go, George," she whispered.

George was still clearly upset. "Marietta, keep that door locked! Nobody's safe anymore. If you have to, call the constable. Keep those ruffians away from our door!"

"Marietta," Muriel tried to keep calm. "We don't have a lot of time, so the beds in the guest room need to be changed, and remember to set up the puddings."

Marietta stood still holding the towel on Peter's arm. The blood was soaking the towel. "I will, mum."

"Don't take any chances." George stopped at the front door, hesitating. He felt uncertain about whether or not he should leave the house. If Sadie and Harold hadn't been waiting for them at the train station, he would certainly have stayed. He looked through the French doors at the ruffians still hiding in the lilac trees and then glanced at Peter and Marietta clinging to each other as they shuffled into the kitchen. "We'll be back soon."

It became so quiet now that Clara grew uneasy in her sleep. Marietta and the wounded Peter left the kitchen and went to Marietta's quarters above the carriage house to find more bandages. When Clara opened her eyes a little, she saw that the room was empty. It was quiet except for the sound of laughter out on the quay. Lifting her head from the cushion on the settee, she realized she had been sleeping for quite a while.

She rubbed her eyes. "Mother! Father! Marietta!"

But there was no reply.

"Marietta!" she called out with anxiety now.

But there was nothing. The dusk seemed crowded around the house as though the sky were blowing the darkness like smoke into all the corners of the yard. The apple trees looked black against the violet color of the water and the brightness of the moon and stars.

Clara had very seldom been left alone, if ever. She had been alone in a room, but there had always been someone in the house. She sat up, startled that she could not bring anyone with her call. She sat for a moment listening, and thinking about what she should do. She might scream. But she was eleven years old.

She knew screaming wasn't good. In fact, sometimes, when she screamed, she got herself into a coughing fit. She decided it would be braver to do something else. Her head was still congested, and she had trouble breathing, but when she saw her music box on the sofa table, she took it down and opened the lid. She decided that even if it hurt, she would rather sing than cry.

Clara went to the French doors and began to sing. She sang to the long grass blowing in the hovering mist, and to the lilac and apple trees. *I refuse to be lonely*, she said to herself. *I will sing until Marietta comes . . . or until my parents come home.*

She sang one of the little songs she had made up to sing with the music box melody:

> *Come down stars, and play with me.*
> *Come down moon, from the apple tree.*
> *You'll be lonely too, I fear,*
> *If you stay there and I stay here.*

She sang it until she invented a couple of other verses for herself—until she was sure that the stars and the moon must have heard her song. Clara liked looking out on the black water, with the boats far away bobbing under their spars and sails. And while she was singing, she did not hear the talking and laughter coming up from the lilac trees. But when she finished the last verse, she thought she heard someone outside the French windows in the dark.

"Pssst."

It sounded like someone was coming across the yard. Soon she was sure there was someone there. It sounded like children laughing, and she thought she heard them mocking her: "Talk to the moon, talk to the stars. She talks to nobody for hours and hours."

She leaned back on the sofa, trying to keep away from the large window, though she could hear bodies jostling one another to look through the glass. Finally, she looked directly outside. A group of both boys and girls were shading their eyes as they looked into the bright room. They were jockeying for position to see her through the window.

"Talk to her! Talk to her," someone goaded the largest boy.

"Oh no, Tom, we shouldn't," a girl's voice chimed in.

Tom . . . Tom must have been the largest boy. He was the leader. A tall lanky fellow with a shock of dark black hair, he had eyes that looked furtively through the glass. Clara had mixed feelings about these visitors. A part of her was terrified. Would they try to come inside? With the light from the room shining on the patio, she could see them clearly. The older boy was dressed in a tattered coat, and there were holes in the knees of his britches.

"She don't want nothing to do with any of us poor folk," Tom said.

"She's so lonely. I bet any of you she'd like to talk to us," a girl chimed in.

"No, leave her alone," everyone said.

Staring at Clara with a strange haunting look, the tall boy named Tom stood at the window glued to the glass. Clara could see his eyes looking directly into hers. His eyes were the largest feature of his face. His cheeks were lean and thin, and his mouth full. He did not say anything for a moment, as though he were seriously thinking about something. "Hey," he said finally. "That house looks like Christmas. How much you want to bet we can all get into that house?"

At first there was a moment of silence—as though what the children heard was preposterous.

"Bet? How much?" one of the others finally said, as though he had his share of experiences with betting.

"What are you going to do? Just kick it down?" The girls shook their heads.

Though Clara could hear the talk and whispering outside the glass, she knew the doors were locked.

"Are we really going to try to get in? I don't think we should try to." One or two of the little children began to run away.

But the oldest boy, Tom, was not shy. He leaned over to the door frame and knocked on it soundly. He kept his face very close to the window. With his nose pressed against the glass, Clara thought he looked like a jellyfish.

"Hey! Tom called out, "open the door."

Clara slipped off the settee and walked quietly to the window. Every child stared at her as though they had seen a ghost.

She guessed that none of them had seen a girl in a white night-gown before. All of them probably had one set of clothes they wore all day and slept in all night. They looked like raga-muffins—hems frayed and big holes in the knees and elbows.

She called through the window first, to let them know she had heard them.

"Open the door," Tom said again.

"My father wouldn't like that," she called out.

"Are you sick or something?" Tom leaned up against the door, getting a good view of her pale face.

"I've been ill."

"What's wrong?"

"They don't know for sure." To make it easier to talk and hear, Clara opened the door a crack. But this was a mistake. Tom was a fairly tough young man. And when he pushed against the door, it swung back. Clara had to skip quickly out of the way. Suddenly Tom was on the threshold. When his eyes rested on the decorated room he stepped back briefly, as though struck by amazement. "Ohh . . . wow!" he breathed.

Brashly, Tom came into the room as though she had invited him. He swaggered in, while the rest of the pack stood at the threshold. "Wow! Macy's windows. Did they buy Macy's windows?"

Clara backed away. "I really shouldn't—"

But it was too late.

Tom had found the music box.

"May I let my little sister see? She loves music boxes."

When he beckoned to the children on the doorstep, they surged into the room. Their jaws dropped, mouths open.

"Oooh. What's this?" They picked up small picture frames on the tables, examined the fireplace, tugged at the holly, and pulled at every ornament on the tree. As they looked at everything, one of them began to stomp in rhythm. And as one person picked up the rhythm, others joined in. They were soon caught up in a strange pounding song and dance. With all of the boys in one line and the girls in another, they stomped on the floor and sang and danced as though they had done it a thousand times before in a thousand forbidden living rooms.

Clara stood up on the stairs to get out of their way. The strange pounding rhythm was something she had never heard before and it began to shake her. But for some reason she was intrigued by it. She felt the vibrations in the floor. She tried to memorize what they were doing with their feet. What *was* it they were doing with their feet? It was astonishing!

"Come here," Tom said, extending his hand toward her. "It's just talk and tap. Talk and tap. Do it. Put your foot here. Hold my hand."

Clara did only a few steps when one of the children called out. "Somebody's coming down the street headed straight for here!" The children ran so quickly from the room that things went flying. The holly came down, and many of the ornaments scattered from the tree. They turned out the lights of the big room and left through the French window to the quay while Muriel and George came through the front door into the foyer.

Clara stood in the light from the quay, in the center of the great room with everything scattered about. Her hair was mussed and flying and her hands at her side were shaking a little.

Still in the front foyer, her father and mother were too occupied for a moment to see her. As she listened to them in the darkness, she thought her father sounded angry. Something was wrong. They had gone after Harold and Sadie, but Uncle Harold and Aunt Sadie were not with them.

"I thought you knew which train it was!" George complained.

"George, I was so sure said Wednesday. Isn't this Wednesday?"

"Well, they're obviously not here, so she must have said Thursday," George said.

"But, there's not enough time! I told them the party was on Friday," Muriel lamented.

"I just wish someone in this house could keep an accurate account of—" George stopped in the middle of his speech as he looked around.

Clara felt her heart begin to beat faster. If he should discover what had happened here, he would be furious. He breathed in and out as though something strange had reached his senses. "Muriel," he began then. "Do you smell something?"

Muriel was busy hanging her cloak and putting away her

umbrella. "Nonsense, George. I don't smell . . . "

George turned to hang up his coat, his back still to the room. "You know, if I didn't know better, I would say some of those filthy urchins had been in this house. It smells foul."

It was at that moment that he left the foyer and turned the lights on in the big room. When he saw what shape his house was in, he backed up. For a moment he couldn't speak. The floor was strewn with items from one end to another. "Muriel!" he cried out. "Muriel! What's happened!" Without stopping to breathe, he dashed in the direction of the kitchen, "Marietta! What has happened!" Turning like a bull in a glass cupboard, he charged about the room, yelling at the top of his voice.

This was the first moment Muriel detected that Clara was still on the settee. She ran to her daughter and leaned over her. She thought Clara was still asleep, but Clara had curled into a ball and pulled the covers over her hair. "George, please! You're waking Clara!"

But George was livid. He would not be stopped. "Marietta!" He reached for the telephone. "I'm going to call the authorities!"

By now Clara was fully awake. "Father, please don't be angry."

"Angry? You're ill! Where's Marietta!" George's chin was quivering.

"Now, George, please. We'll get to the bottom of this." Muriel could do little to calm him down.

"Muriel," George yelled. "You're not going to like this, but we'll have to let Marietta go!"

"Please, George. There's an explanation."

Clara stood up next to her father. She was so small, she was like a wisp of a cloud with the potential of being tossed about by his storm. "They're just from down the street," she said weakly.

"Urchins from down the street!" he yelled. "Living in squalor. Possibly employed by professional thieves! Until we get to the clinic, we don't even know what your illness is, exactly! What kind of outside diseases do these ruffians bring in here?" He turned to dial the phone. "I'll call the authorities."

"George, please!"

He held the receiver away from his face as he railed. But before he dialed, he covered the mouthpiece with his hand. "They broke into our home. There is no telling what damage they have done. Why wasn't the door locked! Where is Marietta! I want this door locked and I want her to *keep* this door locked!"

Marietta could not have helped but hear the commotion. When she came, there were tears running down her face. She pleaded with Mr. Franklin to please understand why she had not been in the room. Peter had been sorely wounded, and she had taken him to her quarters at the top of the carriage house to wash and bandage him. "Please forgive me, sir, forgive me," she cried out.

Assessing her tears, and not hearing any answer at the police station, George slammed the receiver back onto the telephone.

10

On Thursday, the house stayed quiet, as though the storm had passed. Yet Muriel was exhausted from talking George into keeping Marietta. She was so weary from facing one disaster after another that she felt she *must* go out to do some of the shopping just to get out of the house. Though Marietta protested, worrying about the danger, Muriel walked out on the street. If truth be known, she was hoping that she *would* catch sight of some of the little urchins who might inhabit the neighborhood. If she could only look at them she wouldn't have to imagine what had happened. She would know firsthand what her daughter had seen entering their home.

At the corner on the street that approached the waterfront, she saw Liza Felton with a shopping basket bobbing on her arm.

"Liza!" Muriel called. The two women greeted each other warmly. Liza had been invited to the party they were having to welcome Sadie and Uncle Harold.

"I'm looking forward to the dinner Friday night," Liza said.

"I appreciate all your help, though George's Aunt Sadie didn't come when she was expected."

Liza took Muriel's arm firmly, "And how is little Clara, Muriel? Is she getting any better at all? Isn't there something the doctor can tell you?"

Muriel paused before she spoke. "She's still having problems, Liza. The doctor is not quite sure what it is—but it might be asthma. There is a possibility—oh, I can't even say it—that she cannot live here. As the cold weather comes, we still don't know what we are going to do."

Liza was about to answer her, but instead a scrappy little kid with spiked blond hair began tugging on her coat.

"Liza!" Muriel said. "Liza! Someone—?"

Liza turned quickly toward the thin freckled face. The boy was dressed in ragged green coattails, a pair of shredded black socks, and torn-up shoes. His large eyes were the color of two brass buttons. He reached up to her with his long thin hand veiled in a threadbare glove.

This is one of them, Muriel thought. *He was in my house.*

Watching, Muriel felt like putting her hands to her face and covering her eyes. But she resisted, hoping there would be a quick end to these few moments. It was a sight she did not want to see. Her heart began to beat hard.

Liza turned and shifted the basket on her arm.

"Please, mum. Can I have a coin? Me mother's sick and she needs some soup," the boy began.

Liza's look sharpened. She had seen so many beggars at the waterfront, and heard too many stories that weren't true. "What a pretty tale you tell, if I do say so myself!" She leaned over to him and lowered her determined eyes to his. "You want some smokes, don't you?"

The boy backed away from her. But not very far.

"Go home, boy," she said in as stern a voice as she could. "You go ahead home and let your mother know where you've been."

But the boy did not go. He stood his ground as though he had told this same tale a thousand times, as though he had won success repeating this same story over and over again. "Please, mum. It ain't a tale. It's true."

"Scoot. Scoot!" Liza batted him off with her hand as she would bat a fly.

This time the boy did move—and quickly. But before he left he eyed the purse under Liza's arm. It was more temptation than he could manage. He grabbed it away from her.

"Liza, no!" Muriel cried out. "I'll hold your basket! Run!"

Liza tried to run. But with her petticoats and skirts binding her legs, she got only about twenty feet. There was no way she could catch up to him now as he was turning the corner. She called out and pointed to him as she ran, "Stop! Thief!"

Most of the people on the street must not have heard her, for their faces were blank with apathy. When she stumbled over the hem of her skirt, she stopped running, feeling the harshness of the breath that coursed in and out of her lungs. Only one person seemed to be capable of moving quickly—a young man sitting nearby on the stoop of the tobacco store. Dressed in rags similar to the young urchin's, the young man did a double-take when he saw the boy running away with the purse. Sizing up the situation, he turned quickly and ran after him. He must have known the boy, for he called out. "No, Ricky, no!" several times as he ran as fast as he could to catch up with him.

Muriel was sick with worry. "I'm so sorry, Liza. Oh, I hope . . ."

But as the women stopped to lament the loss of the money, they saw the young man from the steps of the tobacco store walking back toward them with a tall man in a dark coat. Muriel thought she recognized the figure! It was the doctor and he was holding the runaway boy by his ear. How fortunate!

Muriel wanted to cheer, but she held her composure. She clung to Liza as they waited for the doctor and the two boys to come to them.

"Haven't I been your doctor for eleven years?" Dr. Kendall grinned at Liza. "I recognize this pocketbook. I remember you knitted it yourself."

The boy was wriggling in his grasp. But he had the purse and he returned it to its rightful owner.

"Oh, thank you, doctor. It was the remainder of my grocery money."

"The boy that ran after this kid? The two are brothers," the doctor glanced at the two boys. "Released upon the mercies of the most compassionate of our society."

Muriel heard his words, but she was not sure what he meant. Without answering, she listened to the oldest boy's impassioned plea.

"Please, Doctor, our mother is sick. Ricky was only trying to help."

The doctor did not listen to the words of the older brother. "I'm very sorry about this." He paused. But he was still holding to the little brother's ear. "This young man owes you an apology."

The boy with the eyes the color of brass stuck his tongue out in an ugly manner at Liza. Turning away, she said a quick goodbye to Muriel and Doctor Kendall, and stuffed her purse deeply inside the basket.

The doctor was a peacemaker in the neighborhood. He didn't press the boy, but smiled kindly at Muriel. "There is no grown-up person to take care of these children," he said. "As a matter of fact, I had one more errand, and I thought I'd have time to check on Clara at your house," he continued.

Muriel looked from the doctor to the older brother, trying to assess the civil distance between them. So there was no adult in these children's lives to take care of them? She wanted to understand. "Thank you so much, Doctor, for what you have done to save my friend's purse. If you're coming I'll hurry along and get Clara ready for your visit," she said. "Come as soon as you can." As she turned back toward home, she could hear the doctor still admonishing the boys.

"What you did was very wrong, son. Don't you know that? Don't you street boys have anything better to do than to help a little boy rob a lady's purse?"

"I was trying to stop him, sir," the older boy pleaded. "He's little. He don't know better."

"He *doesn't* know better," the doctor corrected him. But his reproof fell on deaf ears.

"That's right, sir, he don't know any better."

Suspecting the grammar lesson went over the boy's head, the doctor began on another tack. "Shouldn't you be home? The street isn't the best place to play."

"I'm Tom and this is Ricky," he said solemnly. "I told you, my mother's sick. She needs food, sir. The only way we're going to get it is if we ask somebody for it."

"She's feeling poorly, is she?"

"That lady says you was a doctor? You is a doctor?"

"I am. I *am* a doctor."

"Since you *am* a doctor, might you could help her?"

"You are . . ." Since correcting grammar seemed unproductive, Kendall guessed the boy probably wouldn't comprehend much of anything—even the news that he could not come to take care of another charity patient. How was he going to get out of this?

"First I have important business," he began. And he turned to walk away. There were too many who needed him. But something about the boy's gaze stopped him. Perhaps it wouldn't hurt just to ask them a question or two.

"Boys! Where does your mother live?"

The boys stopped in the road, their shoulders still slumped. "We live in a coal shack on Steel Street."

"Under the viaduct, sir," little Ricky piped up.

With the doctor's pause, Tom tried again.

"Will you come and tell us what's wrong and how to make it better?" he pleaded.

There was something about the depth of Tom's large dark eyes that reminded Dr. Kendall of his own mother's eyes. This child was lanky and lean, with a sunken gray pit above his collar bone. But his thin face was well-proportioned, and his dark brown hair thick and shiny.

The boy's plea was not lost on Dr. Kendall. He turned it over in his mind. Was it at all possible that he could tell the boy what was wrong and how to make it better? After all, he had still not been sure that he could correctly diagnose Clara Franklin's illness. Actually, he had thought it was asthma, but he had been afraid to make a public declaration of it. And if he had known exactly how to diagnose it, it was certainly true that he had not been able to make anything better.

He paused and leaned over to the boy, who was not much shorter than he was. "I can't always tell exactly what is wrong or how to make it better."

"You're the doctor, ain't you?"

Sometimes people needed so much to believe that someone could help them, that a doctor becomes a figurehead akin to God. Some people had little, if any, faith that they themselves held the power to make themselves better. Dr. Kendall knew this, and he knew that if he were resolute, it could rub off on his patients. He wasn't quite sure how to answer the boy's question, but he did hear the word "ain't" and it grated on his ears.

"You're the doctor, *aren't* you," he repeated with firmness.

"No, I ain't the doctor, I know that for sure," Tom said in a serious rebuttal. "But I was hoping you was the right doctor for her, and that you could at least tell us what you think."

Dr. Kendall had to smile. The boy Tom was so serious, his eyes so huge and full of sorrow, that he did not have the temerity to refuse him. "All right," he nodded. "I'll take a few minutes."

Brightening, the boys scuttled along beside the doctor. Tom took his bag, and led the man down the road that lay under the viaduct. The two boys began singing and hitting the road with their feet in a rhythm. Dr. Kendall found the footwork amusing—and, actually—fun.

11

The tracks of the commuter train lay only three blocks away from the Franklin's. On Thursday morning, two figures bundled up in woolen coats and scarves stepped off the train. No one was there to meet them, not even Sadie's nephew George. The empty station put the two a little at odds with one another, though they knew it was their own problem, for they had notified the Franklins they'd arrive on a different day. In the Christmas rush, amidst people going to and fro from New York, no one noticed the pair—a bearded shaggy-haired gentleman wearing a peaked tyrolean hat, and a brightly dressed woman with a fox stole flung about her neck. They were carrying not only small valises, but stacks of brown paper packages that almost completely blocked their faces from view. Barely able to see, they felt their way across the crowded tarmac. They hailed a carriage and dumped their burdens on the seat.

It was Sadie who spoke first in an irritable voice. "If we had come yesterday, we wouldn't have had to take the taxi."

To compound their difficulty, Harold Dosselmeyer misread

the address as 1002, when it was really 1020. When they exited the taxi and gathered all the packages together, the vehicle drove away before they discovered they had to walk another half-block.

"If you had not mixed up the address, we wouldn't have had to walk half a block," Sadie said.

Uncle Harold wanted to say, "Quiet, woman." But long ago he had realized that nothing had ever been solved by being rude. So he kept his mouth shut. Besides, he reasoned, he may not have heard what she was saying, as it was getting harder and harder for him to hear.

In front of 1020 at last, Sadie shouted out to him as clearly as she could, "Is this it? Oh, I think this is it, Harold! Can you see?"

See? Why was she asking him if he could see! Of course he could see. It was his ears he was missing. "I'm hard of hearing, not blind."

Sadie shouted again. "I know you're hard of hearing. But can you see?"

"Eh? What's that? I can't hear you, Sadie."

Sadie gave up. This was the correct address, she knew it, and she didn't need Harold's confirmation. 1020 . . . This was the Franklin's. She began to get excited.

"Oh, I can't wait to see that darling Clara. She must have grown up by now."

Harold's face fell. "You say she must have thrown up by now?"

Harold's legs were tough as a cowpoke's and crooked as a cricket. When he leaned over to hear what Sadie said, he looked like a question mark. But the question went begging.

Sadie changed the drift of the conversation. When she rapped on the door, she reminded Harold: "Now, remember, Harold, Clara is a sick little child for some reason or other. Did you bring that special package for her? Let's make their Christmas cheery."

She did not wait to for an answer. The door opened wide at that moment, and for the first time in their lives they were looking at George's wife and child. "You must be Muriel!" Sadie said.

"Sadie! Harold! How good to see you!" Muriel cried out.

When the pair entered, looking like a stack of brown paper packages, they exchanged joyful moments of greetings, apologies and explanations with Muriel. Harold and Sadie began to feel a little more at ease with George Franklin's wife, whom they had never met.

At once, after dumping the packages on the floor, Harold took a very close look at Clara. "Who is this? This can't be Clara? Have you been keeping a new young lady in your house?"

Clara was at once impressed with Aunt Sadie and Uncle Harold. They looked like old German dolls, with raspy curls and vests stitched and embroidered with flowers and vines. "It can't be Clara!" Uncle Harold said dramatically.

"It's me!" Clara said. "It's me."

By now Sadie had given Uncle Harold his ear horn and he put it up to his ear.

"Eh? What's that you say? It's free? What's free?"

Clara paused.

"Oh," she said. She wondered if this Uncle Harold had understood a word she said. When she moved back, she faltered a little and Muriel caught her quickly and set her down on the settee.

"It's all right," Muriel whispered to Clara. "He can't hear you, dear. You might have to shout." To Sadie, she apologized. "She's . . . been a little under the weather."

Sadie took stock of the child's long face. "We heard about the sickness." There was a long pause. "Well, let's cheer ourselves up," she finally shouted. "Let's give her the present, Harold. Give her the doll."

"Ball? What ball? We didn't bring a ball."

"Well, give her the music box."

"You say she's got the chicken pox?"

From her place on the settee, Clara began to smile. "No," she began. She knew she didn't have the chicken pox.

"Oh dear, Sadie began to twist her hands. "Maybe the seashell, or the feathered hat?"

"She fell where she sat?"

Muriel was beginning to smile, too. "I'm so sorry. She's still a little unsteady on her feet. Sometimes she isn't able to move much."

Harold sidled over close to Clara and gazed as though he knew just what sickness she had and how to make it better. Like a wooden doll dancing on a string, he plunged into one of his large boxes. When he emerged he held a large stiff-looking doll with fuzzy white hair and a handle in back that opened its mouth. Uncle Harold bent close to Clara to ask a question. "Have you ever seen a nutcracker?"

No, Clara had never seen such a doll as this.

Uncle Harold began to dance. He turned in a circle and laughed and picked up his old feet as though he were prancing. "This is a dancing nutcracker from another world!"

"Harold!" Sadie reprimanded him.

"Really! It's true!" he said with excitement.

Sadie didn't think they should tell tall tales. "Careful what you say to the child!"

But Harold didn't hear a word she said. "Everyone knows a nutcracker is a person who comes back from another world to bring joy to people. Especially at Christmas time."

By now Clara thought that both Harold and the nutcracker were the funniest things she had ever seen. Still on the sofa, she began to giggle, and then to laugh out loud. When Harold dropped behind the sofa and held the nutcracker up like Punch and Judy, he raised his voice a few notches and Clara laughed again.

"Hello, Clara!" he shouted. "Now you are what I call a proper little girl. Look at that pretty hair, look at those very bright cheeks. Do you have a special wish for Christmas? I am here to make your wishes come true."

Sadie was about to protest Harold's fantasies again, but she didn't have the heart.

Clara paused. "My wishes will come true?"

"Of course I can't make *all* of your wishes come true, but I'll do the best I can. Do you have any wishes?" As the nutcracker danced on the back of the sofa, Harold bounced him up and down. "I can hear him perfectly. Can you hear him?"

Clara sighed. There was something she wanted, all right. And for a moment she wondered if she dared ask for it. But Uncle Harold was looking at her so expectantly with such funny bulging eyes, she thought she would take the risk to speak. "I wish I had lots of friends," she finally said.

She said it so softly that she would never have expected Uncle Harold to have heard her. But he clicked his heels and responded in a wink.

His eyes twinkled. "Lots of friends," he made the nutcracker talk. "Well . . ."

"What's his name?" Clara asked, watching the bouncing mustache. "Uncle Harold?"

"His name is Harold? Is that what you say? Is that his name? Well, I suppose that could be his name. Hark! Yes, of course! Listen to him speak!"

Clara began to giggle again. "Is he the Harold in 'Hark, the Harold Angels Sing'?"

Uncle Harold sang in the nutcracker's rousing voice, "Hark the Herald Angels sing."

Clara laughed. But she had more questions. "Does he have any brothers and sisters?"

Uncle Harold felt the emptiness in the big room, so in the nutcracker's voice he said, "Yes, I have lots of brothers and—a couple of sisters." He smiled and danced the nutcracker across the back of the settee.

Clara clapped happily. But all of a sudden, perhaps jealous of the nutcracker's good luck at having such a family or, perhaps, because she had not slept much last night, Clara felt very tired. Sitting back in the settee, she curled up in the afghan again, murmuring, "Yes, lots of brothers and sisters. And lots of friends," and she fell back against the pillows.

But Uncle Harold wasn't about to let her fade out of the picture. He continued to sing and dance with the nutcracker until she and her mother could not help but laugh. They hadn't smiled and laughed like this in a very long time. Finally, Uncle Harold put the nutcracker in Clara's arms.

Above the sound of Uncle Harold's songs and the funny nutcracker dance, Sadie and Mother could still hear the ruffians in the street. There was a ruckus out there and Muriel moved to the door to shut it out. But soon a large kick came to the door, and it was pushed open. Muriel gasped at first, until she saw George.

"George!" Muriel rushed to the door.

Mr. Franklin backed into the house with his arms waving.

"Get this rabble out of here, Marietta," he cried, "Get them out of here!" He was shooing the ruffians away from the door.

Muriel hurried to him. "Your Sister Sadie and her husband Harold have come!"

When he turned around and saw Sadie and Harold, he began to break into a large smile. "Sadie! Harold! So glad you made the journey safely!"

Clara was very happy to see her father. She lifted the nut-cracker and tried to rise up out of the settee, but it was too much for her. She fell back into the pillows with the nutcracker in her arms.

Vexed from fighting through the people out in the street, George turned to his daughter and saw the nutcracker for the first time. He paused . . . and then before anyone could say "Jack Robinson," he snatched it out of Clara's arms, surprising every-one in the room.

"What is this?" he asked, examining the nutcracker in his hands. "Toys already for Clara?" It isn't even Christmas yet!"

Sadie rushed to her brother's side. Her tone was a sisterly half-scolding one. "Just a few of them, to cheer her up, George. Come, now!"

It would be an understatement to say that she seemed sur-prised to see George so over protective of his daughter. But of course it was because the little girl had always been so ill. She lowered her voice to calm them all. "How are you, dear George?"

"Toys from the outside . . ." George began as a way of explaining himself, but then he turned to Clara, who had settled back against the pillows. "I am worried about Clara," he continued. I could be better if I knew more about her health."

Muriel came to his side quickly. "The doctor promised he might have some helpful news soon. Remember, he did that other test?"

But George wasn't comforted. Visibly upset about Clara, he began to rant and rave about the fact that they knew nothing about her illness, that the doctor hadn't given them an adequate report yet, and here she was, playing with a toy from a far away land which might have been touched and played with by other children.

"We don't know where this toy has been!" he cried.

Clara sat up in the pillows and tears formed in her eyes. "He makes wishes come true, Daddy."

"We don't know who has played with it. Please, darling, trust me."

"I've already touched it," Clara said quietly. "I want to take it to bed with me."

But Clara's father would have none of it. The laughter and fun with the nutcracker came to an abrupt end. George took Clara's hands and led her upstairs to her room.

12

The doctor had so many patients that afternoon that he didn't get to the Franklins' until everyone in the house had finally settled down or gone to their rooms. It seemed to George and Muriel that they had waited for this most recent diagnosis a long time. So, when Muriel finally saw him in the street, she hurried to open the door.

"You're late, doctor!" Muriel breathed in quickly, hoping she might hear some good news.

"Sorry I'm delayed," Dr. Kendall hung his head. He did not look happy. "I would like to have held this off forever."

"Please come in and sit down," Muriel beckoned him.

But the doctor was too distraught to sit. He did not waste any time getting to the heart of the matter.

"I have the results of the test. It is not good news."

By now George had finished putting Clara to bed. When he came down the stairs and saw the doctor, he stopped for a moment and scowled. "Hello, Doctor," he said, anticipating that something unpleasant was about to happen.

"I *am* sorry," Doctor Kendall continued. "But I think it would be best to get Clara to a drier climate immediately."

"Not good news," George said in a gruff monotone. "But surely you can tell us what the trouble is?"

Muriel held her hand to her heart, afraid to breathe. "Can't you tell us?"

"We are still not sure," Dr. Kendall cleared his throat. "We believe she has a rare reaction to something in this environment which causes an acute form of asthma. Remember, I told you once that the best thing would be to move west?"

George froze. He couldn't speak. He clasped the railing on the stairs.

"I am sorry," Dr. Kendall tried. "I am truly sorry, but it's really the best cure I have for you. I would like to have told you something different."

Muriel held her breath.

Once the initial shock was over, George started to rant and rave again. "This is impossible. We can't just pick up and go somewhere west, like Wyoming or Utah. To live with the savages in a hut or a cave! With Indians or Mormons?"

"I am just telling you . . . the best I know." Dr. Kendall's face looked flushed.

Muriel went to her husband and laid a hand on his arm. "Please, George, we don't have to decide now. At least for a while."

Dr. Kendall looked shaken. "Well, I have informed you. It is just my professional opinion."

As the doctor turned to go, Muriel asked him for tea, but he would have none of it. He had a new patient under the viaduct—an impoverished woman who had just had a baby, he said, and he must get to her.

George turned toward Muriel as she stood at the door watching the doctor move down the steps. When he spoke, he spoke each word in an angry guttural declaration. "It wasn't enough that we could not have any more children. It wasn't enough that she is too sick to play with other children, or ordinary toys. It wasn't enough! How can he even *suggest* we just give up everything we have struggled to build!"

"Please, George, please." Heartsick, Muriel was afraid to face the anger in her husband's voice.

"Leave our home?" he uttered. "Leave everything we have sacrificed all our lives to build?" He knew Muriel could hear him, but he also knew he was really talking to himself. "What is required? How much blood and tears must fall? How can we tear apart our household? How can we bear it all?"

13

he Thursday of Harold and Sadie's arrival had not begun on a good note. Yet, the Franklins knew the party on the following evening would come, and that they must put on happy faces, It would be difficult after hearing Dr. Kendall's drastic measures for Clara.

Muriel tried to calm her husband, but she was also facing her own burdens. As she climbed the stairs with George that evening, she could not say a thing that cheered him. She twisted her hands in the pockets of the robe she wore, and hummed softly to herself, hoping something would save them, but she couldn't imagine what that might be. Being a little acquainted with prayer, Muriel murmured over and over again, "Please, dear God, help us. Whatever is right."

That night, the Franklins slept uneasily. While Harold and Sadie appeared to be sawing logs, Muriel and George tossed and turned in their beds. They weren't the only ones. Clara could not seem to fall asleep at all. Early in the evening, when the street lights were still throwing pools of light on the cobblestones,

Clara got out of her bed and tiptoed down to the stairway that stood over the great room. In the dark, she waited until her eyes defined the settee. She then tiptoed slowly down to the great room and looked in all the places she thought her father might have put the nutcracker. She looked under the sofa cushions, but it wasn't there. She looked on the floor around the sofa, and in and under the chairs. When she stood up, she finally saw it lying on top of the bureau. She ran to it quickly and took it in her arms, holding it close for a long time.

"Please tell me your secrets, Harold," she whispered. "What are they? How do you make wishes come true? Where do you come from? Say you'll stay here and tell me you'll be my friend."

While she was talking in the dark to the nutcracker, a knock came suddenly on the door. Clara froze as she heard voices outside. She held the nutcracker tight, until her hands and fingers began to ache.

"Let us in, Clara. Let us in."

Clara recognized one of the voices; it belonged to the tall boy who had come in with the children the other night. She was sure it was Tom. She held the nutcracker tight and leaned over it, covering it with her hair.

Another sing-song voice yelled: "Tom's got something he wants to tell you. Tom wants to talk to you."

"Clara."

Finally, Clara was sure it was Tom because the voice

sounded sincere. She went to look out on the street. The moon was glowing in the sky, illuminating everything with a silver glow. She stood at the window and put her face up to the glass.

"Tom wants to tell you something," she heard again.

She paused for a moment just to listen. And then she cried out, hoping her voice would be heard. "Let him tell me from there."

Another voice called out, "He can't tell you from here."

"Where is he?" Clara asked through the glass.

"Wouldn't you like to know?" someone said.

"Tell him to come and tell me himself," Clara said.

"Where's your folks? Let us in."

"Quiet," Clara half-whispered. "They're upstairs."

Clara put the nutcracker in the crook of her left arm and held it tight. She considered waking someone in the house, but she wasn't really feeling afraid. She went to the door and opened it a very small crack, but the opening didn't stay small for long. The children grouped around the door, pushed it open, and came streaming in. There were seven, eight, maybe nine of them. And there was Tom. When he brushed past the door, he turned on the lights in the great room.

Clara felt the sound of their voices ringing in her head. "Shhh. You must be quiet. Don't make any noise."

The boys became quiet, but it did not stop them from snooping in all of the drawers and fingering all of the china.

"Is your father asleep, Clara?" Tom asked.

"My father's upstairs," she said in a barely audible voice.

"But can he hear you if you cry out?"

Clara tightened her hands around the nutcracker. She prayed the boys would not try to hurt her, and somehow, she didn't believe they would. She held tight to the nutcracker and made many silent wishes that nothing terrible would happen.

"Well, as mean as he is, at least you have a father," Tom said. But as soon as he said it, he noticed the nutcracker in Clara's arms.

"What's this?" He said, fingering the beloved toy.

Clara felt a tightening in her throat. "My uncle brought this nutcracker from a land far away."

The other boys gathered around. "A nutcracker?"

"See, he talks." She slowly pulled the nutcracker away from the safety of her arm and pulled the little handle in the back of its head. "You see, he can talk to you."

She was not prepared for the reaction of the boys. They began to laugh. Tom's laugh was the strongest of all. "Listen to this, boys. The nutcracker talks to her! Come on Clara, let's have some talk. Talk talk talk talk." Without hesitating, they grabbed the nutcracker out of her arms and began wiggling the handle in back. "Talk talk talk. Would you please tell us what he's saying?"

For a moment Clara thought she might be afraid. But she told herself she could cry out at any time and her father would come. And she was curious what might happen if the children could understand what the nutcracker was saying. Clara knew what he would be saying. She held the nutcracker tenderly and began to whisper softly.

"The nutcracker says he likes you. He says he'll be your friend. He wants to know if you're sad. If there's anyway he can cheer you, then he'll make you feel glad."

Clara believed believed the nutcracker's words were exactly as she said them. But the boys were not buying it.

Tom laughed again. "A talking nutcracker. A rich man's toy. Well, so he wants to cheer me, does he? Make my wishes come true? How about that boys? Are we cheered?"

The boys booed.

"What if we wished for some food?" Tom squawked.

"Yeah. How about he cheers us with some food?" the boys repeated.

Clara looked around the room. Some candy and nuts lay in good supply in holiday dishes around the room. "Sure. He says to take some." The boys ran to the dishes and stuffed their pockets with the treats.

"Are you cheered, boys?" Tom said mockingly.

The boys yelled and snickered. "We're getting that way!" they cried out.

"What if we wished for something to drink?" Tom called.

Clara saw that the hot chocolate was still sitting on the grate.

"Sure, He says there's chocolate by the fire, and you must each take what you want."

As they ate and drank, the boys began to stomp around the room.

"And what about the presents?" Tom sneered.

For the first time Clara felt a strong fear run up and down her spine. These presents were not hers to give. But she did not want to anger the boys. She whispered with hesitation in her voice. "The nutcracker says, take the presents."

Tom stopped as he watched the boys dive under the tree for some of the presents. They put the boxes up to their ears and shook them. But Tom did not dive for any presents. He stopped and gazed for a long moment at Clara.

"Take the presents?" he questioned. "Are they the nut-cracker's presents? Can he give away the presents?"

Clara felt in her bones that she was making the right decision to be generous.

"The nutcracker says to take anything you want. He says he likes you. He wants to be your friend. If there's a way he can cheer you, then he will make you glad."

Tom looked from the boys who were rattling the packages to Clara, to the nutcracker, and back again. "All right, boys. That's enough," he said. He was not laughing. The boys stopped and put the packages back under the tree.

"Those ain't our presents," Tom added.

Clara felt a huge wave of relief flood her heart. She thought she must have sighed audibly. But she didn't hear it, her heart was beating so loud.

"Quiet!" Tom said now. And he peered down to the nut-cracker in Clara's arms and looked at it as though he would stare it down. "Those ain't our presents. And *I* want to talk to the nut-cracker." He looked at Clara. "He doesn't really make wishes come true, does he?"

Clara thought about it for a few minutes. No, there *were* wishes that would come true, she was sure of it. If you told them to the nutcracker, he would help. Uncle Harold said so and she believed him. "Well, he can't make them *all* come true, but he does the best he can," she said, trying to smile just a little. "What would you wish for if you had all the wishes you could wish?"

Tom looked around the room, swinging his arm high. "I'd wish I was rich as sin, just like you."

Clara wasn't aware she *was* rich. She had always been shel-tered from the world outside, and though she had enough to eat and wear, she believed she was like other children who ate food bite by bite and wore one thing at a time.

"We're not really rich," she wanted to protest.

"Oh, yeah? Just look at everything you got. Paintings on the wall, a Christmas tree as big as the stairs, and a sofa as big as a boat."

Clara would have given everything in the room to him in that instant if she thought he would think it was all right for her to be the way she was. "Would you really like to wish for *those* things?"

Tom sneered. "If I wished for them they wouldn't come true."

Clara wondered, but she didn't think the nutcracker gave things like sofas and paintings on the wall. "Maybe that's not the kind of thing he does. Maybe you should wish something special . . . for someone you love."

Tom stood for a moment with a thoughtful look on his face. He held his chin in his hand. "Well, okay," he started. "Maybe I'd wish for my mother to be well," he finally said.

Clara looked at all the children. They were so ragged and out of sorts. Perhaps that was why they appeared as if no one cared about them—their mother was ill. "Do you all belong to the same mother?" she asked.

All the boys laughed.

"No. No. Just my brothers Ricky and Freddy and my sister Julie. And the new baby, Bobby, who is not here, but back in the coal shack on Steel Street. Our father's dead."

For some reason the word "dead" fell heavily on Clara's ears. She sat for a long moment. She had a father that cared so much about her that he was willing to do almost anything for her. "I'm so sorry your mother is sick," she said.

"Yeah. She's sick. But I bet she'd feel better if she saw a house like this," Tom gestured with his arms.

Clara whispered to the nutcracker, who still lay in the crook of her elbow. "Well, what about it Harold?" She put the nutcracker to her ear. "Can Tom's mother come to this house?" At an appropriate interval, she raised her head to Tom. "All right. Yes. He says it's all right."

Tom backed away from her and looked at her with narrow eyes full of suspicion. "No! That is a lie! Listen to the nutcracker talk, boys! Talk talk talk! Sure, come on you raggedy street urchins! Come into our home. Have a visit with Clara's loud father welcoming us at the door!"

Clara wanted to protest. "You never know," she whispered. "You never know."

Tom laughed heartily. "Listen to the nutcracker. So your father's just going to open your house up to a poor woman in a shack with six kids! What a joke!"

Adopting the snobbish stance of a formal butler, Tom said with a cynical grin, "Welcome, Mrs. Hannah Knight. Be one of our guests at the Franklin mansion!" He laughed. "Dress like a millionaire with your children as elegant as beggars! Of course you are ready to inherit the street, and ride in a carriage with silver wheels. 'Look, ma, no hands,' your children say. No heads, either. They have turned into snobs without brains. What a shame, what a shame."

The boys erupted in a collective sneering laugh. They began to shout and scream in rhythm. Tom began to cry at the top of his voice, "These Franklins may have earned their money, but they're poor folk. They're living with a bunch of fancy lies. There's pudding in the cupboard, but it's closed, by Joe. There's fire in the grate, but it's too dang low. They say 'Come and warm your hands, and you can make a wish.' It's all just a pack of fancy lies, and we're better off like we are." He pointed to the boys and the rags hanging around their knees. Tom whirled around with the boys. It was clear that wealth was something he dismissed— or pretended to dismiss, anyway.

"It's friends that make you happy in the end." He sneered again. "These snobs are falling through the cracks of a great big pack of fancy lies. How'd you like to live like that?"

In the center of the room, while Tom and the boys danced around her, Clara stood firm. She had not stood on her feet so long for several months. But she dared not move. When they finished laughing, she said firmly, "I don't think you've given the nutcracker a chance. At least make *some* wish. Wish for your mother to be well and to come to this house to visit. It might come true. But if you don't wish it, it's for sure it won't happen at all."

Tom wasn't fooled by Clara's firmness and he grabbed the nutcracker out of her arms as the other boys began to snatch at it. "Let me give this nutcracker a piece of my mind." He began to work the mouth vigorously. He worked and worked it, until Clara feared the nutcracker would break.

"Start talking, Nutty the Nutcracker. I wish for my mother to be well enough to come to this house just to look at what snobs these people are!"

The boys tussled with Tom to have their own words with the nutcracker. They pulled at it and shouted and screamed and shook it to get the words out of it that they wanted to hear.

Suddenly a strong voice from one of the bedrooms at the top of the stairs boomed out; it was *definitely* not the nutcracker.

"Clara!"

Tom scrambled away from the nutcracker in the center of the circle. The boys stopped shrieking, as they heard the loud voice and dispersed, revealing the terrible result of their rowdy behavior—the nutcracker lay in pieces on the floor. It was no longer a talking toy, but a cluster of heartbreaking wooden fragments.

Clara felt something sick in her stomach. In the misty darkness, she saw her father at the top of the stairs and all the boys slipping quietly out the door.

"Clara! You should be spanked! I would do it, too, if you weren't so sick. Now, be a good girl and get back into bed!"

"I will, Papa," Clara said. But before she went back to her room, she tiptoed over to the broken nutcracker, gathered up the pieces and held them in her arms. Quietly, with tears slipping down her cheeks, she whispered a lullaby to the broken creature who had made her so happy today. "Bye, lullaby, my friend," she sang. She rocked the pieces in her arms and then tucked them gently under a pillow on the settee. Then Clara slid down onto the settee herself, closed her eyes, and went to sleep.

That night, Clara dreamed an unusual dream. She was a princess dancing with the nutcracker. Her father was a villain in a black cloak who tried to pull them apart, but she fought to be with the nutcracker, a true friend. She ran an obstacle course in and out of sugar plum fairies and fireflies as she hurried away from the villain. In the end, the nutcracker took off his mask and Clara couldn't believe it! It was Tom. She was so surprised, she stumbled back and almost fell into a thorny hedge. But Tom put out his hand and pulled her close to him. Like a prince, he rescued her. When she waltzed with him, the lights in the sky skated across the moon like the aurora borealis. There was music everywhere, and the mice and the bears and the Chinese princesses stood in rows along a road strung with globes of light.

15

O ne would have thought that enough had happened on this night before the day of Christmas Eve . . . but, no. Since the nutcracker had been broken, Tom realized he was beginning to care about how Clara felt and he didn't follow the other boys so quickly down the street. He hid in a doorway and watched his friends in the distance as they lay in wait for the Franklin handyman Peter. Ordinarily, Tom would have laughed with the boys, and even approach Peter and trip him up. But tonight he saw that Peter was walking home late with Marietta, the Franklin's maid. Tom hid in the shadows and told the other boys to be still. From Marietta's words, he knew that she was aware of their presence.

"Just don't pay any attention to them," Marietta said in a shrill voice that Tom and the boys could not help but hear. "If you're not carrying any money with you, they won't bother you. They only make threats because they themselves are threatened by the wharf thugs."

She dug a key out of her pocket and opened the back door

to the Franklin home. "Try not to make any noise," she whispered.

While the boys waited in the darkness, they watched Peter and Marietta disappear into the house. Tom told the boys to keep still, because he knew Peter would be coming out of the door again.

Inside, Marietta found Clara asleep on the settee. "Shhh," she whispered to Peter. "We don't want to wake Clara. And we certainly don't want to wake George. George can be furious when I come in late." She hung her shawl on the hall tree and set her hat in the window sill. "George thinks he is the boss of everybody," she added.

When she turned around, Peter took her hands in his. He held them both, tightening his grip around them. "Marietta," he whispered. "Please!"

Marietta waited for a moment, not sure what he wanted to say.

"Why don't you just leave them and come with me?" Peter stood for an awkward moment with her hands still in his. Then he leaned forward and gazed directly into her eyes for a long time. "I love you," he said.

Tom was near enough to the door that he had prevented Peter from closing it. By mistake, his foot struck the bottom of the door, and it opened. Seeing Tom so close, Marietta dashed to the hall tree, picked up her umbrella, and knocked Tom away. Just at that moment—when she was hearing the tenderest words Peter had ever uttered—they had been interrupted.

"Peter! Look out! Get away from him!" she screamed.

Peter backed away from them both. He put both hands up in the air. "Not me! Not me! I don't carry money anymore!"

"Leave him alone!" Marietta cried out to Tom. "Oh, I knew those ruffians were out there!"

But Tom wasn't thinking about robbing Peter, at least not this time. He threw his hands up in the air the same way Peter had done, to beg for peace. "It's just me, Tom. And I've got a deal for you." In a mode of self-defense, he allowed the words to tumble out. "I'll tell those wharf rats not to bother you if you'll do us a favor."

Peter dropped his hands. He stood straight and gazed into Tom's face. There seemed to be something honest in it. He decided to take a chance. "A favor?" he asked. He had never trusted the neighborhood riffraff. But he had always been open to the possibility of being surprised someday. "What kind of favor?"

Tom stepped a little closer. He didn't want anyone in the upstairs bedrooms to hear. The house was so quiet, they could have heard a pin drop. He leaned up toward Peter's ear. "It's the nutcracker. You're handy with a hammer." He stood back. "Clara invited the boys to . . . and I don't want anyone to know it was broken."

Peter stared at Tom. At first he wanted to ask questions. How was it broken? Had Clara allowed those boys to play with the nutcracker? What had she been thinking? But he stopped thinking about the whys and wherefores; he was too interested in what kind of deal Tom had in mind.

"Can I trust you . . . trust your friends?" Peter said as he glanced at Tom out of the corner of his eye.

Tom ordinarily did not make deals with gardeners who worked for rich people who lived in mansions. He was nervous. He stood on one foot and then on the other, and shot a look out to the street where he knew the boys were waiting for him. As anxious as he was to leave, he waited for Peter to understand the transaction.

"You can trust me. Count on it."

Peter repeated what he understood of it. "You don't want anyone to know it was broken."

"That's right," Tom whispered coarsely. "That's my best offer. Take it or leave it."

"Well . . ." Peter drawled. "My place is too small . . ."

"Make up your own mind. You can bring it to our shack on Steel Street to mend it."

Still not sure of what was happening, Peter hung on Tom's words and looked out on the street. It would be nice if Tom called his pesky street gang off of him. "Okay," he agreed.

The young men looked at the pieces of the nutcracker in the still-sleeping Clara's arms, and were afraid to tug it away. Peter wanted to wait until there was a chance she would let go. "I'll bring it by to you on my way home," he said, wondering if he had made a deal with the devil.

Tom spit in his hand and shook hands with Peter, sealing the bargain. When Tom left, Peter rubbed the spit off of his palm and turned to Marietta. She was waiting patiently with the handle of the umbrella still in her grip.

"You can't trust any of them," Marietta whispered on her way out of the room.

It was not easy getting the broken nutcracker out of Clara's hands and into its box. Finally, Peter could not help but wake her up, and he was obliged to tell her that he must take the pieces of the nutcracker because he had made a deal with the boys in the neighborhood.

It had been difficult to get the nutcracker into its box without waking Clara, but it was even *more* difficult getting out of the room with it. There were rumblings upstairs. First, Uncle Harold thought he had heard something, so he came down determined to pick up his ear horn and hear more. Trundling down the steps in his rabbit slippers, he began to search the room. Peter hid behind the couch when Uncle Harold came near and told Clara to throw her blanket over Uncle Harold to distract him so that he wouldn't see the broken nutcracker leaving the place. But, mistaking the two men in the dark, Clara threw the blanket over Peter instead, and when he stood up like an emerging ghost, Uncle Harold was so frightened, he howled and run up the stairs.

By this time, George was certain he heard something and now he came clumping down the hall. With darkness flooding the room, George did not see Uncle Harold. Uncle Harold did *not* see George and the two of them ran smack into each other!

Already spooked by Peter under his blanket, Uncle Harold made a beeline for the stairs howling, "Help! Ghosts! There is something not right in this house!"

George made a beeline for the door, shouting, "Something is going on here! I know I locked that door!"

15

On his way back to Steel Street Tom felt a strange longing in his heart. He had never felt anything like it before. There were many things that were not right about his life, he knew this. He had encouraged the activities of the gang, and he realized he had hurt many people. He knew he had played into the hands of the thieves on Steel Street. Yet, he had always believed what the boys did was necessary, that it was the only way of life for poor people who were forced to live in the street, and that it would never change.

But tonight, as the boys scattered for their homes, he took the long way around. When he approached the gate near his house he could hear the faltering voice of his mother singing softly to the new baby.

> *Bye, lullaby, my little one.*
> *I wonder who you are.*
> *Before you came, what was your name?*
> *Were you far away? . . , How far?*

Many thoughts occupied him. He wondered what had happened between the time he was a baby in his mother's arms and now, when he knew he was the lackey of a dishonest man.

Because he lived in such a small room at his boarding house, Peter decided to fix the nutcracker at Tom's shack on Steel Street. He worked on it while the others slept, from three to five in the morning. When he finished, the nutcracker was repaired so well that no one would ever have guessed it had been damaged. Peter had to go to work at the Franklin home at six A.M. to feed the horses and perform many other tasks, so he left the nutcracker at Tom's home, planning to come back for it in the afternoon.

It was the morning of Christmas Eve, and the day of the Franklin's party. Tom waited with his family for Peter to come back and pick up the nutcracker. It was quiet in the shack on Steel Street and Tom still felt that strange feeling that had developed from spending time in Clara's house. Helping his mother with the chores, he swept up the rocks that had blown over the walkway, cut down the large dry weeds, and chopped kindling. He did not wait for his mother to ask him to clean out the laundry tub and wash the clothes, he just did it. At about noon, Tom was sitting on the floor watching the children play while his mother sat on a crate with the baby in her arms. He expected Peter to come for the nutcracker any moment.

Tenderly, Tom's mother Hannah kissed the baby. "He's our only Christmas gift this year. It will have to be enough," she said softly. She leaned over the baby and let her hair fall over his little hands. She was so weak, it took a great deal of effort to raise her head. "Julie," she called out. Julie was playing in the corner with the boys. They were playing carefully with the repaired nutcracker.

"What, Mother?" Julie said, turning her head to hear her mother's voice, holding the nutcracker in her arms as she sat on the floor.

"Julie, please go to the drawer and get me the little purse."

Reluctantly, Julie got up, but brother Ricky wouldn't let her take the nutcracker. He reached for it and took it from her arms, holding it close to his cheek.

Julie brought the little purse to her mother who checked to see if the little bit of money was still in it. "This is all we have to buy a small amount of flour," she said, . . . "And a few raisins for a small Christmas cake."

It had been money saved for a special purpose. She handed it over to Tom. "Please don't lose it, Tom." Tom took the purse carefully.

"I know, Mother. I won't."

Sluggishly, Hannah looked over in the corner at Ricky still playing with the nutcracker. Julie hurried back to take it from him, and there was a slight tug of war. Hannah Knight realized that as much as she had lectured about quarreling, the nutcracker was now a source of disagreement. She would be glad when it was gone. She sighed to Tom, "Is your friend ever coming back?" She looked down at the box where the nutcracker should have been lying. She hoped the children would put it back in the box where it belonged, but they were enjoying it so much, she didn't want to interfere.

Tom nodded. "He'll be back to pick it up." For a moment he paused. He put the purse down and walked to the children who were playing with the nutcracker. There were some questions he suddenly wanted to ask. He had been thinking all morning about many things, things that puzzled him. But he believed he had finally come up with some answers of his own. At last he felt he could talk to his mother about what he had been thinking and hoping.

"Mother, do you believe in miracles?" he finally said. "Maybe believing is the key." He stroked the nutcracker, though he didn't take it out of Julie's arms. "I think I'm going to believe. I'm going to believe as if it is really true. We'll only have to wait a little while longer and our wishes will happen."

Hannah looked at him, her eyes weepy with tears. "I wish it *were* true," she whispered.

"It is, Mother. Don't worry. Our luck will change. The nutcracker brings good luck."

Hannah dropped her head. "Something's got to happen."

When Tom left, Hannah continued singing to the baby until Ricky tugged on her sleeve, pointing at the purse Tom left behind. As weak as she was, Hannah still knew what was best, and Tom had promised that the ruffian boys of the neighborhood would never bother him again.

16

There had never been such a bustle at the Franklin home as on the afternoon of Christmas Eve, 1917. When the women came on Friday morning to help with the last details of the party, all of them chatted among themselves about what they had learned just a short time ago—that the Franklins must face the decision of their lives— whether or not they would move away to a drier climate.

"My husband says they should move away immediately," Sarah, the doctor's wife said, as she dusted the mantelpiece.

"That's what I heard," Jane shook her head. "I think they're going to Denver."

"Who knows," Sadie piped in. "George seems like the type that will resist *any* move, the whole nine yards."

Muriel, gave directions as they scurried about with the last decorations and some of the last minute food preparations. She caught the worry in her friend's voices as she moved in and out.

"It is a sadness for all of us," she said.

"Maybe you would like Denver," Sarah said to Muriel.

"You'd like it if Clara got well," Marietta said encouragingly.

"I think that is the answer," Aunt Sadie said in a burst of enthusiasm. "If Denver will make Clara well, then everyone will be very happy."

Sadie and the other women moved out of the way when Uncle Harold came down the stairs in his starched shirt looking for the nutcracker. "Where is the nutcracker?"

Because she was in charge of many things, Muriel hardly knew how to manage it all at once, much less keep track of the nutcracker. "I told Clara not to take it upstairs. But I don't see it," she said as she moved out of his way.

At that moment, Clara came to the top of the stairs. All of the women bustling about the room stopped for a moment to look at the pale little girl in her white nightgown.

"Clara, dear," they said, almost in one voice, coming to her to wish her well.

Only Muriel seemed determined to get things moving again.

"Clara," she asked, "did you take the nutcracker upstairs, dear?"

Clara did not want anyone to know that Peter had taken it to put it back together. And she especially didn't want Uncle Harold and Aunt Sadie to know the nutcracker had been broken. Clara didn't want to lie to her mother, either, but she did not want to tell the truth. "I'm sorry, Mother," she said softly. Her answer satisfied her mother, and it was an honest answer.

For no one was sorrier than Clara that she had let the ruffians come in and play with the nutcracker until it had been broken almost beyond repair.

Sadie, standing by, seemed to be ready with a solution for every problem, and especially for her husband. "You'll have to sing your song without it, Harold!" she quipped. Immediately Harold broke into the nutcracker song,

"He's the nutcracker, he's the nutcracker."

The women in the room stood back and admired the dance he did in his pajamas. At that moment everyone looked again toward the stairway, for George had come down.

"Ahem," George cleared his throat to stop the activity in the room. He looked imposing in his ascot tie. He was buttoning down his cuffs with a pair of pearl cuff links.

Clara turned to him a little worried. "Hello, Father."

George was not in the best of moods, but then, he had almost never been in a good mood. During the night he had been awakened in the early hours of the morning . . . several times. And now the scowl on his face was situated between *angry* and *pleasant*. "It's a wonder any of you got up at all. I thought I heard noise all night. Did you get any sleep, Clara?"

"Yes, Father," Clara answered.

"You're ill, remember? You should be in bed."

But Clara had hoped to make this last day in New York one she could remember forever. "Can I stay up for the party, Father? Just for a few minutes?"

"Of course not," George said without hesitation.

Like sensitive antennae in the room, the ladies understood that they were extras in the middle of something that might turn out to be unpleasant. Because they had almost finished their work, they gathered their things quickly and made many excuses to be gone.

"Goodbye, Muriel," Jane curtsied to her friend. "We'll see you this evening."

"We've got to be going, Muriel. I'll bring the cakes," Sarah hurried.

"We'll be back to help," Jane promised.

When the women left they almost bumped into Peter on the walk. He smiled at them and nodded. He was carrying the nutcracker box with a small blanket spread over the top of it. He walked into the house and called out, hoping to find the family home, but by this time Muriel had gone to the kitchen, and George had ushered Clara up the stairs to her room. Only Marietta, on the way to the kitchen, had seen him coming. Still carrying the box, Peter smiled to see Marietta coming back into the room quickly, wiping her hands on her apron.

"Hello, Peter. Come in."

But Peter already *was* in.

Peter was curious about what the Franklin family was going to do. "Well, what's the verdict?" he asked Marietta. He set the nutcracker box down on the window seat. "Are they going or staying?"

Marietta looked at the stairwell, hoping George would not hear anything. "Who knows. Of course George says it will happen over his dead body; and no one wants to discuss it in his presence, especially so close to the party."

Peter shook his head. "Still trying to make a party happen when they should be following the doctor's orders!"

Marietta stopped, looked down, and shook her head. "You don't know him like I do. He is just amazingly stubborn."

Peter was feeling very heady today. It was almost Christmas. And he had just won asylum from the hoodlums in the street. He felt like speaking his mind. "What does that have to do with you? Get a new position!"

But Marietta did not react to his demand as he guessed she would. She stood with her hands on her hips and looked straight at him with a bit of a snarl in her voice. "Peter, it's always *me* get a new position. Why don't *you* get a new position? I can't leave them now! Don't you see? Clara is too sick. She needs me."

Peter actually couldn't believe what was coming out of his own mouth. "That's what I thought, Marietta. They own you. And he's such a grouch."

Marietta didn't blink when he said what he did about George, although it *was* very bold. "Well, maybe he's a grouch," she agreed with him. "That much is true. But they don't own me. I'm choosing to stay with them."

Peter realized he would have to take a different tack. He reached for her and held her hands. "Marietta," he said in his most serious voice. "I need you. I need you as much as Clara needs you."

Marietta didn't answer for a moment. She looked Peter up and down. "Did you repair the nutcracker?"

"Yes, I did," Peter was proud to say. "Though what I'd really like to repair is Clara. If she weren't so sick, you could leave their employ. Don't tell me no, now, Marietta. If Clara was well you'd go with me . . . wouldn't you?

Marietta softened. "I suppose so."

Peter took her in his arms and she didn't resist him. He put the palm of his hand on her cheek, and leaned close to her face. He held her and danced with her around the room as she swayed with him. "I love you, Marietta. You know that! So let's think about it. All right?" He elaborated with a few bars of a song. "We'll have a place all our own, you and me. A little shanty by the deep blue sea. 'Cause we'll be livin' on love."

Marietta felt the whirl of that dance for the next few moments. She stood by the bureau and caught her balance. Outside on the walk she could see Jane bringing back the cakes to the party. "Quick, they're coming for the party," she whispered. "I've got to get to work. But you can come in the kitchen and help me." Peter thought he would probably followed her to the end of the world . . . not to mention the kitchen.

17

*S*uddenly the great room was full of people for the Franklin's Christmas party. Uncle Harold descended the stairs, still in his rabbit slippers. Although he finally had pants on, his Christmas outfit was not complete—no tie and the suspenders were still unbuttoned on his socks. But he was in fine fettle when he caught sight of the nutcracker box on the window sill. He began to crack his heels together. "Well, it looks like the nutcracker's back again! Now I can crack those nuts I was hoping to crack, eh?"

Aunt Sadie followed him in. "Now you can sing your song again!" she exclaimed.

With his suspenders flying, he leaped up in the air and knocked his heels together. "He's the nutcracker, he's the nut-cracker. He can crack a nut with style. If you want him to, he can talk to you. And you'll crack a smile."

He made a fine figure bouncing around in soaring sus-penders, but Aunt Sadie thought she really ought to get him to finish his dress. "Harold, it's time to get your clothes on."

Uncle Harold cocked his head. "Eh?" Perhaps he hadn't heard. "I have clothes on!"

"Fasten your Christmas hose and put on your coat and cravat."

"I'm not fat. Really, I'm not that fat."

"Dress up! Finish dressing up for the party!"

"What party?"

Aunt Sadie gave up. "You're hopeless. The big party. The one we came for. You know. If they move away, this may be the last party we can come to."

Uncle Harold must have heard something, because he began up the stairs. But he left mumbling, "I've got clothes on. I don't see what you mean get clothes on. If I was naked I could get clothes on, but I am not naked. Am I? No, I'm not naked. I have clothes on."

Uncle Harold disappeared just in time, for Sarah, Jane, and Liza were at the door now in their party dresses, bringing dishes of the remaining party food. Muriel came to the door with open arms, and then she and Marietta took the ladies' dishes into the kitchen.

"It's made according to your special recipe, Muriel," Jane exclaimed.

"You will love this dessert, Muriel," Sarah exclaimed.

This time the husbands were accompanying their wives, and Jane's husband went to the phonograph with a special cylinder he had brought to play for the Christmas season. With the music filtering out over the great room to the twinkling lights of the tree, the guests began talking with one another. Some of them swayed to the rhythm of the strings. There was a freshness in the air—of pine and good food, and the happiness of good fellowship.

Liza's husband Gregory, however, finally noticed George had not yet appeared.

"Where's George?" Dr. Kendall also asked.

"Yes, I was wondering where he was."

Muriel knew. She had left him in the upstairs room talking on the telephone to Denver. Though she was hesitant to say so, she revealed George's whereabouts to Dr. Kendall.

"He is on the telephone to Denver, and could not be interrupted. The bank in Denver called to talk to him, but he hasn't made any commitments so far. He's just spent his time yelling at them."

Sarah, close by, overheard her. "He won't move?"

Jane moved to Sarah's side. "Is it as serious as all that?"

Muriel put her finger to her lips. "I shouldn't have said anything. We mustn't mention it."

When the cylinder of music stopped, they all looked up to see George standing at the top of the stairs.

There was no question about it—George was an imposing figure. Dressed in his tuxedo, he was tall and good-looking, his hair slicked back against his head, and his dark eyes alert not only to every beat of the music in the room, but to the silence, and to everyone's mindful attention.

There was a moment of absolute silence while he looked down at the guests. No one knew for sure what they expected to hear from him. Were they waiting to find out if he had accepted the job in Denver? No one breathed a word, or dared to say.

"Don't let me interrupt anything," George finally said. "He waved his hand.

Only Muriel was brave enough to answer him. "Oh, yes, George. We were listening to Gregory's new phonograph recording."

Gregory came forward. "Yes, it's really quite nice. Do you want to hear it?

No one moved.

"Of course I want to hear it," George finally said. "Put it back on." He waved his hand toward them benignly. "Do your dance to it."

"Wouldn't you like to join us?" Jane spoke up.

"Go ahead, all of you! Please!" George so much as commanded. "Please go ahead. Enjoy yourselves. It's a party!"

Everyone really did try to be full of Christmas cheer, although it came off a little stiff. The women began to move their skirts, as Gregory put the music back in the phonograph.

Almost ready to dance again, suddenly everything stopped. Somewhere in the room, no one could be sure where, there was the distinct cry of what sounded like a small . . . child.

George was at the bureau pouring himself a drink, when he

raised his head and heard the cry. "What was that?" he asked Muriel.

The cry came again.

"Am I hearing right? I thought I heard a child . . ."

Muriel began to worry profoundly. "It sounds like a baby, George. It sounds like a baby."

Everyone in the room began whispering to one another. It might have been a trick, but it definitely sounded like the cry of a child.

George had suffered enough for one week and this time he could not hold back his anger.

"A baby! Why should we be hearing a baby! It's got to be on the street! The guttersnipes in the street! I can't believe they would torment us like this!"

He turned to Muriel in exasperation.

"What's going on, Muriel?"

Muriel put her hand on his arm to calm him. "It's all right, dear. Calm down. We have guests."

Jane put her hand behind her ear. "I think that baby is close," she whispered.

George went to the window seat to look outside at what he thought might be a trick played upon them by the hoodlums of the neighborhood. He heard the cry plainly below him. It was coming from the nutcracker box! He leaned over and ripped the nutcracker blanket away from the top of the box.

"What is this!" he cried out.

There was a hush. Everyone gathered around George. The baby stopped crying.

"George, no!" Muriel hurried to his side. "George, no! What *is* this?"

"What is going on, Muriel?" George could not believe that a small baby was moving its hands and feet inside the nutcracker box. He just could *not* believe what he was seeing. He had just yelled at the bank in Denver, having received the dictum that the doctor suggested they move so far away he would have had nothing of his present life with him in any way, shape or form. His daughter was insolubly ill. He was not used to such traumatic disturbances. And now he had come home to enjoy probably the last social event he would ever know in New York City, and he must give it over to the presence of a baby on his window seat? This was not going down well.

Muriel did not hesitate. She took the baby out of the box and put it in George's arms. The child stopped crying.

"You see, it's quiet in your arms, George. I will get some milk." Marietta followed Muriel to the kitchen.

George seemed to grow a little subdued as he held the child.

"I thought it was the nutcracker box."

Peter could not hide any longer. "It *was* the nutcracker box, sir."

George glared at him—though the sharpness of his glare had blurred as he gazed at the little child breathing softly his arms.

"Trust you! I might have guessed *you* had something to do with this, Peter."

"Uh, no," Peter tried to explain. "I thought it was the nutcracker, too, sir. I repaired the nutcracker at the little shack on Steel Street under the viaduct. When I finished it, I brought it here."

Uncle Harold may have been hard of hearing, but he had managed to hear Peter's words about the nutcracker. "Huh? Somebody broke the nutcracker? Ohhh, it'll never be the same again."

Now it was Sadie's turn to try to calm her man. She put both of her hands on his shoulders. "Calm down, Harold. Keep your head."

"Eh? Eat my bed?"

Peter interrupted them with words of assurance.

"It's all right now, Uncle Harold. I fixed it."

The guests in the room seemed to have been holding their breath during the entire scene. They began to breathe, now, unsure of what to do while the drama unfolded. Someone suggested putting the cylinder back on the phonograph when something else suddenly occurred. A white face appeared in the window, and there was a knock on the glass.

George took a step back, shocked by this sudden appearance of a face in the window. When the figure had made itself known, it moved away from the window and to the door. Marietta looked around at the guests. She was as fearful as anyone else to answer the knock, but she stepped forward. After all, it was her duty in the Franklin house to answer the door.

When she drew the door open, the entire room gasped. A small woman in rags stood shivering on the stoop. She was sickly pale, her hair snarled about her head. Her cloak was full of raw tears and holes. She had no socks, only a pair of large brogans on her feet. And she had clearly been crying. Her cheeks were raw with rubbing, and tears still stood in her eyes.

George hurried to the threshold "Don't let her in!" he gasped.

Muriel put her hands to her mouth and let out a sad sound of protest. "She is so cold, George!"

"You want disease in this house?" George yelled, even though the child was still in his arms. "You just want the entire neighborhood to bring whatever they have into this house?"

"George! It's Christmas!" Muriel cried out.

The woman carried a bundle in a large sash on her belt. Carefully not touching the bundle, she stretched her arms forth toward George, and the tears began to course down her cheeks. "Oh, I am so sorry!" I am so sorry," she cried. "Please forgive me!" As she stepped across the threshold, she took the bundle from her waist. When the cloth fell away, everyone in the room saw the nutcracker. "Please forgive me! It was a mistake!"

Uncle Harold's mouth opened until his jaw seemed to drop to his chest.

"Oh, my goodness! So *there* is the nutcracker!"

He went toward it quickly and snatched it away from the

woman, holding it high over his head. He began to click his heels. "Unbelievable! Unbelievable!"

The woman did not wait for anyone to invite her into the room. She lunged forward and lifted the child out of George's arms.

"Oh, thank you. Thank you so much," she cried.

For what must have been the thousandth time, she rubbed a soiled hand on her cheek, yet the tears continued to fall.

Muriel came to her and put an arm around her.

"How long it has been since we had a baby in this house!"

The woman began to unwind the nutcracker blanket from the baby.

But Muriel stopped her. "Aren't you Mrs. Knight from down by the viaduct? You must keep the blanket. And you must come in and get warm, and have some food."

George looked on with worry in his eyes.

"Muriel! Muriel, I need to talk with you," he began.

There were a dozen people standing around who had done nothing to stop the woman from entering the house, and as George looked around, he realized he was alone.

Hannah stepped down into the room and stopped suddenly. It was as though the lights in the room had crowded over her. Her eyes seemed to suffer from overwhelming shock. At first, the neighbors standing in the room surprised her. She had seen some of them before, others she had never met. And then her eyes followed the tall ceiling of the great room to the cornice painted with beautiful roses. She sighed without knowing that she sighed.

"Come in, Mrs. Knight," Muriel repeated. Seeing that Hannah Knight was shivering from the cold, the other women came to her and gave her a shawl from the closet. They helped her get the hair out of her eyes.

"Oh," she whispered, looking around at the dresses, the lights, and the faces of the people. "I can't stay. I'm so sorry for intruding on your party."

No one in that room had been present when that special request of the nutcracker had been made by Tom—that his mother might come into this beautiful house. Not even Tom's mother knew of the wish. But it was true that the fresh smell of the evergreen garlands, the lights on the tree, and the turkey cooking in the kitchen made such an impression upon Hannah Knight, that her eyes brightened significantly. By the time Jane tied the hood of the cape under her chin, Hannah's face looked almost beautiful.

"How beautiful you are," Sarah said cheerfully. "Come and get some food to take to your family."

No one had been aware that by now Clara had come down the stairs and opened the front door. Tom and the other children came quietly into the room, almost unnoticed.

Having heard Sarah's words, Tom swaggered into the room.

"Her family is here," he said importantly, boldly entering the room as though he had been invited and everyone had been waiting for him to come to the party. The guests were so surprised, they were speechless, but not Tom. He had heard Sarah's comment, and he came straight to his mother and confirmed the observation. "Mother," he said, standing only a few feet away, and leaning back as though he must get a good perspective to express his opinion. "Mother, you truly *are* beautiful in this house!"

Tom's words seemed to jar George from his preoccupation of amazement.

"Muriel," he said quickly. "I need to talk with you! Now!"

With the neighborhood support around her, she was finally brave enough to speak her mind.

"Please, George! You're not listening!"

He stepped back, surprised at her resistance.

"I'm not listening? So this is my problem, is it?"

While the women fussed over Hannah, Tom went to Clara.

"I'm so sorry about the nutcracker, Clara," he said.

Clara's eyes sparkled. Her cheeks looked full of color against the white of her gown. She smiled as the children came in, and then smiled at Tom.

"I'm glad you came, Tom."

Though he still seemed to be in a trance, George was not oblivious to everything. He saw the look the two children gave each other, and his face began to swell and change color.

"What is going on here? I can't believe you would condone this, Muriel. Clara! You're going to bed right now!"

Forcefully, he placed himself at Clara's elbow and pulled her to the stairs. She was not able to resist his determination. But Muriel moved Clara aside and stood between them. She knew she had an entire room full of people who would agree with her.

"George, it's Christmas Eve," she said firmly. "Everyone! It's Christmas Eve! Let's have some fun. Start the music!"

When Greg put the cylinder into the phonograph and the children heard the waltz music, they looked at one another in wonder. Some of them had never heard such music before. George had begun to climb the stairs, but gradually, he could see that the merriment of the crowd had triumphed over him. He stopped on the steps and watched people begin to dance the waltz.

But the surprise of the evening was still to come. Tom picked the needle up off the cylinder and shouted, "You call that dancin'? Come on, kids. Let's show them!" And to the tap of their feet, the street kids spaced themselves out across the great room and stomped and danced their own brand of dancing. They danced and danced, the little girls bouncing their skirts, and the boys throwing their arms out, sitting on their legs and giving Russian-style kicks with their big shoes.

George was appalled. And even Muriel stood twisting her hands in her apron. But both of them noticed a warm smile on Clara's face. At the end of the stomp, Muriel began clapping. The others in the room joined her, and the adults smiled and laughed, saying, "That is certainly a different kind of dancing! You have to be very nimble for that kind of foot work."

Muriel noticed that from his point of view, standing on the second step of the stairway, George looked like he was beginning to consider reserving his judgment.

"That was delightful," Muriel said. "Wasn't it!"

The guests continued to clap with great enthusiasm.

"And now, let's do more!" she smiled and approached Tom. For a moment the room fell quiet. "Tom, may I have this waltz?" She was smiling. No one said anything. It was dead quiet while Greg put the cylinder back into the phonograph and applied the needle. Graciously, Tom raised his arms to hold Muriel in the dancing position.

For a few moments Muriel danced with Tom to the waltz music in Greg's cylinder on the phonograph. Something wonderful happened. The other guests in the room chose a child, or Hannah herself—even with the baby in her arms—for a whirl around the room in the waltz. As they whirled and twirled, the children began to laugh and giggle. One of them stopped the waltz music again, and pulled some of the guests with them into doing their noisy kind of dancing. The guests who had the courage to try the new steps began laughing and exclaiming, "How fun! Why, I believe this kind of dancing is fun!"

It was Tom himself who finally walked to the phonograph and put the waltz music on for the last time. When the waltz began, he came to Clara. He offered her his hand and pulled her away from the stairs where her father still stood, dumfounded. He pulled Clara to the center of the room and began to waltz with her. Clara, moving easily with Tom's lead, let her feet glide over the carpets. She twirled, letting her head swing back. She was entirely light on her feet, and swinging with abandon to the waltz, smiling in Tom's arms.

When George finally saw the two young people dancing so happily with one another, he came out of his hypnotic daze.

"I'm sorry!" he cried, pulling the two young people apart. "We've had quite enough!"

Clara and Tom stopped, with George standing between them. "We can't have another moment of this! We're trying to have a Christmas party! This isn't a charity ball for the riff-raff of the neighborhood. This has gone on long enough!"

He put his arm around Clara and, determined, pulled her up the stairs.

"Clara, you are going up to bed!"

He took one last moment to look back at the children dancing the waltz with the guests in the room.

"As for you hoodlums, you are going back to your places on the waterfront. Please take yourselves out of here!"

There was dead quiet. No one dared to make a sound. The father of the house had spoken and he turned to follow Clara up the stairs.

Suddenly Clara, leaning against the railing ahead of her father, began to fall. In a split second, her hand on the railing was no longer visible. She collapsed against the stairs. Everyone in the room quietly gasped for breath.

George was frantic. "We let this go on too long!" he shouted. "I knew it!"

"No!" Muriel cried. "No, Clara, no!"

But in the quiet of the room, there was another voice that came forward.

"Make way. Let me see her. Let me see her!" It was the doctor.

He came quickly, climbed the stairs, and knelt at her side. "Oh, Clara, darling," he said fervently. "Oh, Clara, darling, you were having such a good time!"

t this point, the party was virtually ended forever. The guests left quickly with the painful realization that things had not gone well for the Franklins. There was a feeling of dread in the big house on Christmas day. Harold and Sadie surprised everyone by insisting they must leave. They assured Muriel and George that they had loved meeting Clara, and they had immensely enjoyed the party, but they felt that with the seriousness of Clara's health problems, it would be better to be on their way back to Bavaria. They would take a carriage through the park to the railroad station, and they hoped George would write to them again soon.

After ranting and raving, George finally decided in no uncertain terms that he and his family must go immediately to the west to take care of Clara's illness. There was nothing else they could do. They had come to the last knot on the rope.

There were empty trains available on Christmas day that would not be available on the day after Christmas when everyone else would be traveling to their homes. Now feeling under terrific pressure, George Franklin ordered the household to pack, to get going, to move quickly. There was no time to be wasted. He *would* follow the doctor's orders. He had been derelict in his duty. The bank in Denver was ready to take him. *Get going* were his new words of resolve.

But *get going* also became a sore mantra for Marietta. She had much too much work to do in too short a time. While Muriel and George packed in the rooms above, Marietta brought some of the kitchen packages to the front door. When she saw Peter outside the door, she was happy to see him, but she also felt too pressured to talk to him right at that moment.

"Marietta!" he said. "I need to talk to you."

He followed her back into the kitchen.

Marietta walked with a determined step, her head high. "I've got so much to do. I've got to finish packing and cleaning," she said. Her head was beginning to ache.

But Peter wouldn't let go. He looked around at the packed bags.

"I can't believe the old grouch finally decided to go. And so quickly. *And* on Christmas day!"

Marietta glanced at him with a sorrowful look. "They had to do something quick because she collapsed so suddenly at the party last night."

"Is she well enough to travel now?"

Marietta paused from her work, stacking and carrying items back and forth.

"No matter what, they're determined to go where she'll be well."

With the slightest hesitation in her step, Peter caught up with her. With an exaggerated gesture, he stepped around in front of her. "Marietta," he said firmly. He was not asking a question. He was making an announcement. "You're not going to Denver with them!"

In the middle of tying up one of the bags, Marietta raised her eyes to his. "I'm not?" It surprised her that Peter sounded more confident than he had before.

"Marietta, I have something to tell you. I found a position." He emphasized the word "position," and grinned with glee. "I'm going to repair the clockworks at the foundry!" At the word "position," Marietta stopped tying the ties on the bags.

Of course Marietta had no idea what repairing clockworks would be about, but she stopped for only a moment, and then pressed forward to continue with her work.

Peter watched every move she made. He hoped what he said would have an effect. "And now that I have a way to take care of you, I'm asking you . . . will you . . . I'm asking you . . ." He was stumbling. But just a little. "Will you marry me?"

Marietta raised her head. Her eyes popped open. "Oh . . ." she managed to get out. "Peter!" It took her a moment for the news to sink in. But then she forced her eyes shut and looked away. "Marry you? Oh, I couldn't . . . I couldn't . . ." She looked about and waved her arm over the room, over the kitchen, over the house, over the life the Franklins now so quickly must put away.

"I couldn't leave them! They need me!"

Peter saw something flicker in Marietta's eyes. He believed she loved him. She did. He knew it, and he would prove to her that it was the right thing to come away with him.

"Marietta! Say yes! Please say yes to me!"

Alone, without her family in America, Marietta had always believed there was only one course of life ahead of her. She had guessed she would probably work as a servant in someone else's home forever. She gazed around the house. This had been the perfect place for her. She had her own bedroom above the garage. She had taken Muriel's old sewing machine up the garage stairs and learned to mend curtains, sew doilies, dresses, and even hats. Muriel had been like a big sister to her. Clara was an angel. Yet she had to admit that she had always dreamed of having her own home.

She gazed at Peter with a blank stare. *Could she?* she asked herself. Could she be happy trading the Franklins for Peter? She loved Muriel, that was true, but she had never liked working for Mr. Franklin, who had often allowed his anger to flare up until he hurt others. But perhaps Peter was different? Here he was standing now, waiting for her answer.

Marietta smiled. Finally she held out her arms. She believed she could give him a qualified "yes." If she could leave George Franklin forever, it might be worth it. Yes, she might be able to go. But she did not know how George would take it. She felt she really could not stand one more temper tantrum from Mr. Franklin. That's when she thought that perhaps she could leave the Franklins if Peter would accept the task of telling them. If Peter would break the news, it might be all right. "Maybe I'll go with you, Peter, but you'll have to be the one to tell Mr. Franklin. I just couldn't do it."

Peter was not sure she said yes. But he was feeling very powerful at the moment. He reached for her and held her in his arms. They danced across the room—that is, until they saw George looking down on them. There he was at the top of the stairway buttoning his cuffs. "There are three more suits to pack, Marietta," he said, with his eyes on the buttons. Finally, when he raised his eyes, he saw Peter in the room. "Hello, Peter!"

Even as she watched George at the top of the stairs, Marietta dreaded how angry he might become if only he knew that she wanted to go with Peter.

Trying to be brave, Peter began with another topic of conversation. "Oh, hello sir. I see you decided to go to Denver."

George may have been dressed in nice traveling clothes, but he hadn't yet put on his best behavior. "Did I have a choice?" he snarled.

Peter began, testing the waters. "Sir . . . I . . . I just arranged to take a position, sir."

Marietta stood by, cheering Peter on. But he could sense her anxiety. She probably had a good reason to suspect that he might never come out with the news to George Franklin. And both of them were wondering what kind of volcano would erupt when he *did* understand what they were trying to tell him.

"That's nice, Peter. Get those bags, Marietta," George quipped.

"Now, Peter," Marietta whispered.

But Peter saw a need and his generosity just could not stay concealed. "I'll help with those bags," he said. And he picked them up to haul them out the front door.

"Hurry," George said to Marietta on his way out to the carriage in front. "We've got a lot to do our last night here." As he left he muttered, "I can't believe we're leaving on Christmas day!"

Left with Peter in the room, and without the situation resolved, Marietta just about broke into tears. "We can never tell him."

But when Muriel came in at that moment from the kitchen, carrying bags with towels and kitchen utensils in them, she could not help but notice that Marietta was almost crying. Putting the bags down, and gazing at Peter and Marietta, she demanded to know what had been going on.

"I'm . . . ah . . ." Marietta stammered. "I'm not sure, ma'am. But . . ."

Peter finally stepped in. "Sorry Marietta can't come with you. You will be all right in Denver with the Indians. They can help you. I've asked Marietta to marry me."

For a moment there was a pause. Muriel looked from

her maid to the boyfriend several times. Finally, she put her arms around Marietta and held her for a long time. When she pulled away, there were tears in her eyes. "Oh, Marietta! How wonderful! I'm so happy for you!"

By this time, George had returned to the house. In his anger, he did not sense that anything special had happened. He was busy with one goal, and he was pressing toward the results of their decision to go. "Don't stand there! Get her bags!" he yelled.

"Marietta . . ." Peter began. But he didn't get very far.

"Peter, I have to get their bags," Marietta said weakly.

But a strange miracle took place. Peter, in a way, became George. He was now as determined as George had been, and to prove it, he began to shout. "Hold those bags!"

Marietta pulled back, puzzled. Peter had become someone she had never seen before. She couldn't believe it. It struck a little fear in her.

"Peter! You're angry!" She was now looking at him as though someday she might be the source of some of that anger.

Peter yelled, "I'm not angry."

It was just like George to deny it!

Muriel looked at Marietta. Marietta looked at Muriel. Muriel smiled and put her arm around the girl. This was one of those revealing moments in life that usually occurred *after* the honeymoon. But it was happening to Marietta in this moment, and Muriel was going to coach her through it with a little bit of good humor.

"Being a woman is different from being a man," she grinned. "Picture the world, if you can, if we were the same."

Marietta relaxed. There was Peter, acting like a big bear. And George was growling, too. There was no need for it, and Muriel, who had years of experience, could tell Marietta a thing or two about it. She grinned and held Marietta fast to her. She leaned over to whisper in the girl's ear. "Men are made following a separate plan. They are top heavy, ready to fight or swear. They move down the road trying to make sure nothing will stop them. That's their life's work, you know. To be frightening enough to protect us from anything that might get in our way."

Marietta nodded, trying to understand.

The room seemed to be boiling with inexhaustible energy. Because Peter wanted Marietta to stop working now, he carried the bags out himself. George continued walking back and forth checking parcels and adding extra items. Soon the men had gone out of the room in what seemed like an exaggerated flurry. Marietta and Muriel still held to each other, when they noticed that Muriel's friends, who had come to help with the packing, were standing, laughing, at the door.

Muriel had to laugh at the looks on their faces. They were completely amused at the antics of the angry men. Sarah clapped her hands at the scene. "They are a bunch of blowhards!" she grinned.

Watching, Jane began to giggle. "Sometimes you just have to live with it."

"By the way," Sarah wanted to know, "didn't you say that Sadie and Harold left already?"

"I did," Muriel said.

"But I just saw them in a carriage at the park," Sarah hesitated.

"No, I don't think so. When Clara got so sick, I think they thought they were helping to get out of the way," Muriel said.

"Well, I'm glad you're still here!" Sarah gave Muriel a one-armed squeeze.

"We just wanted to say goodbye," Jane smiled. "How is Clara?"

Muriel seemed to lose her enthusiasm in a heartbeat. When the girls gathered around her, and her thoughts had begun to focus on Clara, she hung her head as the tears began to well up in her eyes. "She almost died."

The girls soothed her with soft words and gestures. But they could not seem to stop the tears from falling. Muriel looked around to focus on their faces.

"It's all right. Don't try to say anything," Jane held her close.

But Muriel wanted to talk. "I'll miss the house, yes," she began. "But most of all I'll miss my friends. I'll miss all of you so much!"

Looking at one another, the ladies continued rubbing Muriel's back. "We'll write a postal card. You can always come to visit us."

"You'll just have to believe that everything in Denver is going to be what you dreamed of."

Muriel shook her head.

"Maybe Denver will be wonderful!" Jane tried.

"The air is so pure," Sarah bent close and tried to smile. "Surely Clara will get well in one of those mountain retreats where the buffalo roam and the antelope play. I think you might love it, Muriel."

Muriel might have said something, except that Peter and Marietta and George came back in. The girls, as though on cue, stepped out of the way.

"I think that's all of it," George was still in a roaring mode. "Except for your bags, Marietta."

Marietta meekly began to explain, since Peter hadn't been able to do it, that she wasn't going to be putting any of her bags on the carriage. "Sir, Peter and I are trying to tell you . . ." but her voice trailed off into an inaudible sound.

Having dried her tears, Muriel stepped forward. "Father, Marietta's not going." It was as simple as that.

George stood very straight. He cocked his large dark head. "Marietta's not going with us?"

Muriel breathed a sigh of relief. He had it right.

"I will never forget your kindness, sir," Marietta stammered to George.

Peter began to click his heels, so ecstatic about receiving a form of permission—even though sudden and questionable.

"Oh thank you, sir. Thank you."

"Did I have a choice?" George said.

"Please, George," Muriel continued. "They're going to be so happy."

George seemed dumfounded. So much had been happening in the last few days, that he was numb with the rapidity of the changes. "I hope so," he muttered. But he could not bring himself to rejoice in their personal fortune. He had too much on his mind. He seemed dazed as first the friends, and then Peter and Marietta left them in the empty house.

In the quiet room, Muriel took her husband's arm. "You know, they all leave you sooner or later," she whispered.

There was still enough strength in George's anger to come back with an argument. "Not all."

Muriel believed she knew what he meant. "I didn't mean Clara," she said.

"If Clara . . ."

He might have said the word "died," but Muriel put her fingers on his lips. "Please, George. Please don't say it. She still has a chance. We must put that hope foremost in our thoughts— that in Denver she will get well."

George had planned most of his life. He had arranged his work so that he would make enough money to support his family. He had worked diligently to achieve everything he had ever wanted. He was accustomed to making things right. He believed that Clara *would* be well because he was taking her to Denver. He would protect her from all harm, and the world would respond with generosity and love. The great God in the heavens above who loved them all would answer their prayers favorably if they did all they could do. Clara *would* get well. He would see that it happened that way.

But when Muriel pulled him down beside her, she began to talk in a way he had not heard before. "George," she began. "Even if she gets well . . ."

George was not sure what she wanted to say. But there was something on her mind that she hadn't ever told him before. "Even if she gets well, George . . . someday, even if she's well, she'll grow up and leave us . . ."

George turned to Muriel. He believed his wife was the most beautiful woman in the world. And he hadn't thought much about it lately.

"Someday she'll leave you," Muriel whispered. "One day she'll walk away. True love will be letting her go."

True love is letting her go. George had never heard it said that way before. He had never thought of Clara as a woman someday. And yet it was only a few years away. He closed his eyes— because he wanted to envision Clara as a young woman, and to believe that she would still be his beautiful little daughter.

"Someday she'll find love on her own," Muriel whispered. "But she'll always be a part of our lives. And she'll know that we will always love her."

19

*I*t was only a few hours later that George and Muriel, who were trying to stay steady with the series of events changing their lives so rapidly, heard a loud knock on the door. They were still packing boxes and getting some of the kitchen goods tied up in string.

When they opened the door, they did not seem surprised to see Tom. Behind him, lurking in the shadows of the porch, were several of the neighborhood children.

"I heard you were leaving," Tom said. "I want to see Clara."

George seemed beside himself. The presence of the children was just one more nagging event to cause frustration. And he had been tried enough. He would never allow Clara to come to the door to see the children.

"Impossible. She's still sick," he managed to say, but in his vexation, he turned away from them and gave the problem over to Muriel.

Muriel's voice was quiet and disciplined. "She's so very sick, Tom. It will be all she can do to get on the train to Denver."

Tom stood on one foot and then the other, leaning into the house, but staying politely in the doorframe. "Denver? That's far away."

"Yes it is . . ." Muriel began with compassion.

George looked numb.

But outside the house on the walk there was a sudden disturbance among the children. Muriel leaned forward when they pointed, laughed and cried out. "Hey! Look who's here! Peter and Marietta! And Clara's Aunt Sadie!" one of the children called. "And Uncle Harold!"

Indeed! Peter and Marietta had returned. "Look who we found outside just as we were leaving!" Peter cried out. "They missed the train!"

Alert, George managed to go to the window. Yes, it certainly was Aunt Sadie and Uncle Harold! Muriel started toward them! She had no idea how they had arrived at this particular time. "Sadie and Harold!"

"Well, as usual," Sadie said good-naturedly, "we miscalculated!"

Harold began nodding; his head bobbing up and down. "I too just palpitated!"

George seemed dazed. He shook their hands, but he let Muriel do the talking.

"Sadie and Harold!" Muriel smiled. "We're glad you miscalculated. We tried to tell you, you should have planned to spend more time with us!"

"Well, we wanted to help by disappearing," Sadie said.

"Yes, we thought we could help by kissing, cheering," Harold grinned from ear to ear.

When Muriel let Uncle Harold and Aunt Sadie into the room, George tried to stand as a sentry to keep the children out on the street, but they slipped past him and began to disappear into the empty corners, or among some of the bags and boxes. Still, George did not shout to stop them. It was as though he had shouted enough and he was letting things take their course now. A few other visitors who had come to wish them goodbye were also standing outside of the door and had come in when everyone else came in. They were Muriel's friends. One of them was the doctor, who came with his wife Sarah. And at the back of the group, behind the children, Muriel saw the little mother Hannah Knight, with her baby in her arms. Muriel went to her to welcome her in.

The room seemed crowded now, and George had begun to look the other way—until all of the children began to gasp. As the children looked up, it grew quiet in the room. Everyone looked toward the white light at the head of the stairs. It was Clara.

The children, and all of the visitors, lifted their faces as little Clara, in her white gown and gold hair stood clinging to the railing on the upstairs landing. "Hello, everyone," she smiled.

Without a false step, she walked down the stairs.

"Clara!" It was George. He ran to her. "You mustn't! You're much too sick, honey! No, sweetheart!"

As he dashed up to her, the doctor came forward with his wife Sarah. The doctor climbed the stairs. "George," he cried out, "let her come down."

George stopped abruptly and gazed at Dr. Kendall.

"Let her come down," the doctor repeated. "I think it may be the best thing for her."

Clara was still smiling. "Merry Christmas, everyone!" she called out.

"Clara . . ." But George's voice had grown weak.

"I wanted to say goodbye," Clara said. But it was not goodbye that was on her lips. "Hello, Tom." She looked at the young man and waved her fingers.

Tom came as close to the stairs as he could. "I came to tell you the nutcracker made my mother well."

Tom's mother Hannah did not hear his words, for she and Muriel seemed to be absorbed in conversation.

"It did?" Clara said.

"The wishes . . . they came true."

Clara leaned against the railing on the stairs. "Oh, Tom! They did? The wishes came true?"

The children had gathered around Tom and Clara. With her father at her side, she began to introduce the children who were standing about in the room.

"Father, these are my friends: Sally, Sara, and Bobby, Amy, Priscilla, Steven, Danny and Freddie. Dori and Sophie."

A tiny girl stood at George's knee and began pulling at his

trousers. George leaned down to her and looked in her eyes. "And what's your name?" he asked.

"Julie," she said.

Uncle Harold began to circle the group of children. He walked around them and around them several times. At first he murmured to himself, but slowly his voice grew stronger and stronger.

"It came true! That's what she wished for. Don't you see? These are her friends. It came true! She wished for lots of friends."

The doctor walked to the group and stood over them, assessing them carefully as though they were part of a hospital staff. "George," he said, "this is most amazing! I've been observing how much improvement she shows in the presence of her friends." He fidgeted and stood to the side with his chin in his hands as though he were thinking, and thinking hard.

"I told you it was necessary to go to Denver. . . " he drawled. "But . . ."

"We're ready to go to Denver," George declared.

No one noticed Muriel in the background with Hannah. But she had heard the doctor's words. For she came up through the crowd leading Hannah by her hand. She laid her other hand on George's arm.

"You're not listening," she whispered to him. "The wishes, they have come true."

"What is he trying to say?" George seemed puzzled.

"I heard him. I heard what he was saying," Muriel said.

The doctor smiled at Muriel. "I'm trying to say that I think we have finally seen the problem. And maybe the cure. It may not be necessary to go to Denver after all."

"We're—" George began.

"You're not listening," Muriel tugged at his arm. "Listen to what he's saying, George. We may not be leaving after all . . ."

Then Muriel turned to Hannah and took the baby into her arms. "Hannah just told me she would be willing to take Marietta's place! And how much better it would be if the little family lived in the carriage house instead of the shack on Steel Street!"

George pulled back. "Stay? Is this a joke?"

Sarah stood by her husband. Dr. Kendall was a patient doctor. He was still smiling when he tried to explain to George for the second time what he had seen today.

"No, it's not a joke. I am aware of cases just like this one in medicine. I think she's just been very lonely. You've been so eager to protect her, when what she needed most of all was right outside the front door."

Everyone in the room was dead quiet. There was not a sound. The tick of the clock sounded like a kettle drum.

"Of course, if you still want to move to Denver . . ." the doctor said.

"Oh no," Muriel made her own wishes known immediately. "I made a fervent wish." She held the warm little head up to her cheek. "The wishes have come true. We can live in our home."

"Of course living at home is where one should live! Forever," Sadie piped up. She had a smile on her face as broad as her face was wide.

"I can't believe what I'm hearing," George exclaimed. "Can this be true, Muriel?" he gazed at Hannah. "And someone to take Marietta's place? Unbelievable! Why didn't I see this myself?"

Muriel looked around the room. The lights were warm, and Clara was smiling and laughing with the children. She could not hold back the feeling of gratitude in her heart. She rocked the baby gently in her arms. Again she repeated, "All my wishes are coming true!"

George gazed at the crowd in the room. He could easily remember his years as a child without access to anything so beautiful as the room and the smiling faces in the room. He knew what it was like to be alone. He knew what it was like to be hungry.

"And mine too," he whispered. So they are!" He looked at the children. Today, suddenly, on this Christmas day, they had become individuals instead of the general face of poverty.

Without precedent, George leaned over to Muriel to whisper to her. "He does seem to be a bright young man."

No one had expected George to call Tom to him, but he did. He beckoned to the boy. Surprised, the young man responded quickly.

"Tom, when I left the bank yesterday, one of the managers said he was in need of a sweeper. Would you be interested in doing that kind of work?"

Tom was wary at first. But George's voice warmed him. "Work at the bank, sir?"

"Yes. He needed someone who would work hard, cleaning and running errands. Do you think you could handle such a position?"

Tom did not waste time being demur. "Oh yes, sir. I could, sir. I would be very good. Yes, I will."

The small girl who had introduced herself as Julie came and took hold of George's trousers again. In some language of the heart, she had understood what George had done for her brother. This time she was close to Clara, and not afraid to speak her thoughts, "You have a very big father, Clara," she said. "He looks like a nice father, too."

George looked down. The girl was so tiny she was practically lost to him. He moved to the side so that Clara could come to the little girl. Clara held the nutcracker in her arms. She leaned down to Julie and said, "And now that the nutcracker is well, he can make your wishes come true."

"I'm glad that the nutcracker is well, now," Julie said.

Tom knelt down to her. "Julie, do you have a wish?"

For a moment Julie looked around at the faces in the room. Everyone was watching her, and she ducked back next to Tom.

Tom smiled and put his arm around her. "No, make a

wish, Julie," he whispered. "Make a wish that will be one of the greatest wishes of your heart. For the wish might come true."

Julie still hedged. Even though Tom was beside her, and Clara had knelt down close to her, holding the nutcracker in her arms, Julie could see all the people in the room, and she looked from face to face nervously.

"I wish," she began. She ducked her little head, and with her chin down, she could hardly be heard. "I wish I had a nutcracker."

The crowd in the room heard what she said. They looked at each other with perplexed faces. What they did not see was that Uncle Harold had caught Clara's eye. He was grinning a grin as broad and wide as a cheshire cat. He nodded to Clara, a nod of permission, of gladness and smiles. He nodded that there was something she could do, and he wanted her to do it. The language they spoke to each other was the language of love.

Clara lifted the nutcracker from her knee and put it lovingly into Julie's arms. The little girl put her arms around it and held it next to her cheek.

"Clara, you are such a good friend."

Tom rose up and waved his arms about. "We are all friends," he shouted. "We're friends!"

The children milled about in glee, being careful not to touch anything.

And Marietta and Peter, though they were about to take their baggage with them in a taxi, went one last time into the kitchen and brought out cookies and hot chocolate for everyone.

"How's your Christmas?" Uncle Harold sang. "If on friendships we rely, we don't ever have to say goodbye."

★ ★ ★ ★ ★

From that Christmas on, it was a different kind of neighborhood. The children did work in the yard in exchange for small favors. Marietta and Peter came to bring their children to play. Sadie and Harold returned from Bavaria every year with another nutcracker. And the children of the Knight family grew into responsible adults who, following George's example, worked hard and took good care of their families.

Clara and Tom? George taught Tom to work hard at the bank, and one day several years later, they got married and had a large family of their own.

And what about George? He learned to give and take a little better. He and Muriel were both happy when the new little baby moved into the carriage house. And, with all of the Knight children and their children and their grandchildren, and his *own* grandchildren in the family of Clara and Tom . . . George and Muriel finally had their many children after all.